Key Processes in Strategy

In the dynamic environment of the 1990s, a new emphasis is emerging in strategic management. There is a realization that certain processes are directly linked to competitiveness, and that these key processes are an essential part of strategy. Organizational capabilities are now being seen as at least as important as market positions in the development of strategy and the building of enduring competitive advantage.

Key Processes in Strategy explores innovation, learning, structuring, leadership and culture, and transformation and renewal, and examines their links with competitiveness. Leavy takes a harder look at the so-called 'softer' variables in strategy, from the perspective of the management process analyst but with support from economic theory. The approach is thematic, combining a strong grounding in practical questions with a range of theoretical perspectives.

The book is presented as a thematic companion to a case-based approach to teaching strategic management, and will be of interest to educators working at senior undergraduate, MBA and executive development levels.

Brian Leavy is AIB Professor of Strategic Management at Dublin City University Business School.

Key Processes in Strategy

Themes and Theories

Brian Leavy

INTERNATIONAL

THOMSON
BUSINESS PRESS

Key Processes in Strategy

Copyright © 1996 Brian Leavy

First published 1996 by International Thomson Business Press

ᵢⓉP A division of International Thomson Publishing Inc.
The ITP logo is a trademark under licence

British Library Cataloguing-in-Publication Data
A catalogue record for this book is available from the British Library

Library of Congress Cataloging-in-Publication Data
A catalog record for this book is available from the Library of Congress

First edition 1996

Typeset by Routledge
Printed in the UK by Clays Ltd, St Ives PLC

ISBN 0–415–11466–7 (hbk)
ISBN 0–415–11467–5 (pbk)

International Thomson Business Press
Berkshire House
168-173 High Holborn
London WC1V 7AA
UK

International Thomson Business Press
20 Park Plaza
14th Floor
Boston MA 02116
USA

Contents

Preface

It is now widely accepted that we are living through a time of revolutionary change in the general business environment. However, not only is the overall context for strategic management radically changing, but so too is our basic understanding of the nature of strategy and competitiveness. For many today the primary route to sustainable competitiveness is through the building of distinctive capabilities rather than the selection of market positions. Building competitive capability requires, among other things, a fundamental understanding of certain key processes of strategic significance.

Helping to provide that understanding to students of senior undergraduate, MBA and executive development programmes in strategic management is the primary objective of this book. It is intended to be a thematic companion to support the case-based teaching of strategy. The emphasis is analytical rather than prescriptive, and the book should help to stimulate debate in the classroom rather than pre-empt it. It should also be a useful resource to many business executives who, seeking to update themselves, are interested in a concise, up-to-date review of some of the most fundamental concepts and issues in the strategy field. Finally, it should prove to be a valuable resource to students searching for interesting dissertation topics in the strategic management area, because it highlights throughout many of the debates and questions currently energizing the field and includes an extensive bibliography.

Acknowledgements are due to many people. I would like to thank David Wilson of Aston University for his encouragement at the initial stages of the project, and Rosemary Nixon and Gabi

Woolgar of Routledge for their backing and support. My production editor, Angie Doran, and the rest of the Routledge staff involved with the book, including my copy-editor, Emma Waghorn, have all been a pleasure to work with, good-humoured, supportive, and thoroughly professional. I would like to thank my dean at Dublin City University Business School, Anthony Walsh, for helping me to create and protect the substantial amount of writing time needed to complete the project. Some of the research for this book was carried out at the HEC in Montreal, thanks to the hospitality and friendship of Yvon Dufour and the goodwill of Marcel Côté and his colleagues. A special word of thanks is also due to my students at DCU, and at the Carlson School of Management in Minnesota (where I have been a visiting teacher on the MBA programme), who provided the lively and stimulating crucibles within which, over the years, the idea for this book took shape. Finally, I would like to thank Ailish, Emer and Eoin, and the rest of my family, for their support and encouragement, always.

B.L.

Chapter 1

Key processes – themes and theories

The strategy field as a self-conscious discipline is just over thirty years old. It had its early roots in the publication of Chandler's *Strategy and Structure* in 1962, Sloan's *My Years with General Motors* in 1963, and the PIMS (Profit Impact of Market Strategy) research, initiated within General Electric, and still continuing to provide useful insights right through to the present day (Schoeffler *et al.* 1974; Buzzell and Gale 1987).

STRATEGY OVER THE YEARS

Over those thirty years there have been many developments in the field. Among the main concepts developed during the 1960s and 1970s were the product life cycle, the experience curve, the strategic business unit (SBU), and the growth-share (portfolio) matrix. The Boston Consulting Group, under the leadership of Bruce Henderson (1973), was the dominant influence. The 1980s were dominated by the contributions of Michael Porter (1980, 1985, 1990) in the industry and competitive analysis areas, including the five-force model, generic strategies, the value chain and the diamond. The 1980s were also characterized by a strong interest in strategic change and transformation (Quinn 1980; Kanter 1983; Pettigrew 1985). These developments reflected the enormous growth in interest and research effort in the field since its early beginnings. They also reflected the changing shape of the strategy problem over time (Ansoff 1979). In the more benign international economy of the 1960s and 1970s, the emphasis was primarily on strategies for growth, and strategy became almost synonymous with diversification and vertical integration. During the low-growth 1980s, the emphasis in the strategy field shifted towards competitiveness and renewal, particularly in core, and often mature, businesses.

There is a growing belief that the business world in the 1990s is facing a whole new set of priorities. Deregulation, new information, manufacturing and materials technologies, and the increasing globalization of competition, are all contributing to an unprecedented level of dynamism and volatility throughout the international economy. The 'rules of the game', and the engines of future economic growth, are believed to be changing in very fundamental ways (Beck 1992). In this new environment, large vertically integrated companies will no longer dominate industries as they used to. Companies will compete on the basis of not only their own capabilities but also those of their suppliers and allies. Information technology is tooling the new industrial revolution. Knowledge workers are the key resources, and the horizontal coordinating of processes rather than the vertical control of functions will be the new emphasis in the structuring of organizations. These developments are changing the nature of business and competition in fundamental ways.

A NEW EMPHASIS ON THE STRATEGIC POTENCY OF KEY PROCESSES

Since the early days, many courses in strategic management, in both academic and executive programmes, have been divided into two distinct sections or modules. One, dominated by economic analysis, typically deals with the formulation of strategy (industry and competitive analysis, generic strategies for the single and multi-business company), while the other deals with aspects of the management process largely concerned with the implementation of strategy (structure, measurement and reward system, resource allocation). In this traditional model the role of internal processes was clearly seen as subordinate to product-market positioning, and as a lower-level activity that was attended to, as it were, 'after strategy'.

In the dynamic environment of the 1990s, a new emphasis has emerged. There is a growing realization that certain key internal processes are directly linked to company competitiveness, and are not just subsidiary to strategy but part of its very essence. This recognition started with the 'excellence' crusade of Peters and Waterman (1982), and their 'back to basics' assertion that execution is strategy. It was also fuelled by the growing influence of researchers such as Quinn (1980), Mintzberg (1987) and others, highlighting the inadequacies of the traditional two-stage model, with its tendency to separate analytically the thinking and action stages of the strategy process. More recent developments in the competitiveness literature have provided further impetus (Prahalad and Hamel 1990; Stalk *et al.* 1992; Hammer and Champy 1993). In an economic environment where product life cycles are shortening, technologies are converging, and industry structures are becoming increasingly volatile and diffuse, strategy is being seen to be less about the selection of markets and market positions, and more about the building and nurturing of key internal capabilities that are relatively enduring. Increasingly, sustainable competitive advantage is being seen to be rooted in a company's ability to innovate, learn, leverage relationships, implant vision and renew. In short, the centre of gravity in the strategy field has been steadily moving away from the 1980s preoccupation with external industry organization and market structure to a 1990s emphasis on internal processes and competencies. As Rumelt *et al.* (1991: 22) recently put it, 'both theoretical and empirical research into the sources of advantage has begun to point to organizational capabilities, rather than product-market positions or tactics, as the enduring sources of advantage'.

At the conceptual level this new emphasis has already been reflected in the recent rise to prominence of the resource-based view of the firm (Wernerfelt 1984; Barney 1991; Conner 1991; Grant 1991; Mahoney and Pandian 1992; Peteraf 1993), to challenge the traditional dominance of the industry organization (IO) perspective in strategic analysis. The examination of a number of key internal processes and their links with strategy and competitiveness will be the primary focus of this book.

THEMES AND THEORIES

In exploring these key internal processes and their links with strategy, the emphasis in the book will be on themes and theories, rather than on any single underlying framework. The treatment is organized in this way because the concept of strategy remains a complex and eclectic one. Even after more than three decades, the field still lacks a central paradigm or unifying theory (Whittington 1993; Prahalad and Hamel 1994). Developments in strategic management remain practitioner-led, and the most influential conceptual frameworks, right up to the recent notions of core competencies and capabilities, still tend to emerge from the attempts to codify best practice. Grounding the teaching of strategy in case discussion is still the most favoured approach, despite some recent scepticism (Mintzberg 1990). Even the resource-based view, the one theory that is 'unique to the field of strategic management' (Peteraf 1993: 179), is necessarily limited as a potential paradigm. As Porter (1991: 108) recently remarked, the resource-based view cannot be a self-sufficient theory of strategy because the 'stress on resources must complement, not substitute for, stress on market positions'.

The strategy process cannot yet be fully understood in terms of any single integrated framework, and none is offered here. Strategic management 'as a field of inquiry is firmly grounded in practice and exists because of the importance of its subject', and not because of its theoretical coherence (Rumelt *et al.* 1991: 6). As an academic discipline the field has been an inveterate borrower from the older more established disciplines like economics, psychology and political science, right through to the present. It is still perceived as largely theme-driven or question-driven rather than theory-driven. For example, in a recent survey of prominent researchers the strategy field has been variously described as an 'eclectic forum' where 'people trained in various fields come to grapple with problems relevant to top managers', and an arena where researchers tend to pursue 'a research question wherever it leads', spanning functional areas, crossing levels of analysis and looking at 'a lot of theories along the way' (Meyer 1991: 821–31).

Reflecting the state of the field and its strong applied nature, the overall approach to the examination of key internal processes will be thematic. The emphasis will be on trying to take a harder look at some of the so-called 'softer' variables than has generally been done in strategic management texts to date. The examination of these themes will be carried out in 'conversation' with relevant theories and debates, as Mahoney and Pandian (1992) might put it, in order to give the treatment some real analytical bite. The focus will be on trying to understand how key processes like innovation, learning, leadership and culture are linked with competitiveness and economic performance. The overall perspective will be that of the management process analyst, but with support from economic theory, drawing on, for example, the transaction cost branch of organizational economics (Barney and Ouchi 1986; Rumelt *et al.* 1991), and the 'Austrian' non-equilibrium tradition on learning, change and innovation (Jacobson 1992).

THE OVERALL STRUCTURE OF THE BOOK

The book is primarily intended to be a thematic, thought-provoking companion to a case-based approach to teaching strategic management. It has been written with a liberal use of practical examples, so that it can also be a resource for the reflective practitioner. It does not pretend to be comprehensive in its coverage of the strategy process. It veers towards a resource-based emphasis, not as an alternative to traditional industry analysis but as a complement to it. The industry analysis area in strategic management is already well supported with suitable analytical companions. The same cannot yet be said for the key internal processes most closely related to competitiveness and economic performance. The book is intended to fill the gap between the dedicated single topic analysis and the more comprehensive strategic management textbook, in which these key processes still tend to receive relatively minor attention.

The five key processes that form the main body of the book have been chosen to reflect the 'major shift in the basis of competition' being wrought by the 'silent industrial revolution' already in train (Prahalad and Hamel 1994). They are innovation, learning, structuring, leadership and culture, and transformation and renewal. Understanding these processes is felt to be key to a more complete understanding of the strategy process in today's more dynamic conditions (see Figure 1). Since these processes are interrelated in the practical world, there will inevitably be a degree of cross-current in the analysis as the treatment unfolds. Though no comprehensive framework for integrating them exists, there is a guiding logic that has linked them in the mind of the author, and this is reflected in the chosen order. The capacities for innovation and learning are felt to be among the primary sources of difficult-to-imitate capabilities at firm level, particularly in this era of time-based competition. Fully leveraging such capabilities, using the new tools of the information age, will involve the capability to develop and manage new structural arrangements and networks of relationships within, and across, organizations. All three will require a deep appreciation, and some fresh appraisal, of the links between leadership, corporate culture and economic performance, and meeting the challenges presented by the new economic environment will involve substantial transformation and renewal for most established organizations.

The general thrust of the treatment is non-prescriptive. The primary intention is to help broaden perspectives, through highlighting some of the central questions and debates that still engage strategic management research and practice. The thoughtful student or practitioner can then make these insights more fully their own through grounding them in their own case study analyses and discussions and/or practical experiences. In using the book as assigned reading, teachers will still find plenty of scope to ask their students 'What do you think?', and to offer their own particular perspectives on many of the issues raised.

Each of the five key processes selected for examination has its own dedicated chapter, though some interrelations among the

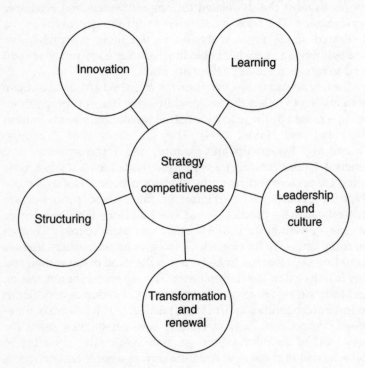

Figure 1 Key processes in strategy

processes are explored along the way. The book ends with some final reflections on the terrain covered by the overall analysis. It does not attempt a comprehensive integration; such a task is likely to remain a mighty challenge in the strategy field for many years to come. However, it notes the strength of the cross-currents among all the key processes featured, which were much greater than had been expected when the book was originally planned and the writing began. This was particularly true of learning, which had very strong links with all the other processes. The thematic analysis as a whole also revealed the strong duality at the heart of strategic management – its rational (Mr Spock) and romantic (Captain Kirk) nature – (something that rarely if ever tends to come through with much force in other strategic management textbooks or thematic companions), and the overall treatment closes with a discussion of this duality and its implications for the future of the discipline.

Chapter 2

Innovation

We begin this examination of key processes in strategy with a look at innovation in organizational settings. One of the central and enduring themes in the management of the strategy process is illustrated in the popular Harvard Business School case of PC&D Incorporated (Hamermesh and Christiansen 1976). In the case, company president John Martell is faced with the prospect of losing three of his best people to the allure of starting up their own enterprise. Martell introduced the concept of the entrepreneurial subsidiary into PC&D to help keep his enterprising talent in the company. It was an imaginative response that turned out to be an administrative nightmare. The central questions raised in this classic case are still current and universal. How does the established company go about retaining and developing its capacity for innovation and enterprise beyond the start-up phase? How does it institutionalize this capacity in a way that will survive the tenure of the founding entrepreneur?

There is little doubt that these questions are now becoming more acute than at any time in the past. The capacity for innovation is being seen as increasingly crucial in the context of the emerging 'new economy'. 'To innovate is to survive', claims Nuala Beck (1992), while Tom Peters (1990, 1991) warns today's companies even more imperatively to 'get innovative or get dead'. Furthermore the link between innovative capacity and sustainable competitive advantage, even survival, is increasingly seen to depend on a company's ability to bring new products to market faster than anyone else. One of the most devastating examples of such time-based competition was the motorcycle war between Honda and Yamaha in the early 1980s. When Yamaha expanded capacity to become the world's largest manufacturer of motorcycles, an accolade that its major rival had always cherished with intense pride, Honda, in retaliation, turned its resources to the new product development process. By bringing new models to market at the rate of almost one per week for over a year, the company made its rival's range appear so old-fashioned and jaded that Yamaha sales plummeted. The episode ended with a public apology by Yamaha for having the temerity to challenge Honda's number one position (Morita 1986; Stalk 1988). In short, innovative capability is now seen as central to sustained success. According to the entrepreneurial founder of Microsoft, Bill Gates, 'cleverness' rather than 'scale' has become the critical competitive factor in his industry, which is one of the main engine rooms of the new economy (Rebello *et al.* 1993: 51).

Traditionally, many companies and management experts have looked to the process of formalized corporate or strategic planning as the best way of trying to institutionalize the entrepreneurial activity within the mature firm (Ansoff 1965, 1987). Steiner (1979: 10), for example, was quite explicit in explaining that 'in a fundamental sense' formal strategic planning was 'an effort to duplicate what goes on in the mind of a brilliant, intuitive planner'. Other experts were more circumspect. Argenti (1980: 30) believed that corporate planning, in the hands of a team of managers, could not 'compete with the entrepreneur' in terms of innovative capability, but should at least 'protect a managed company from failure'. Since the early 1980s there has been growing disillusionment with the capacity of strategic planning to deliver on these promises, and growing disenchantment with the very notion of formalized strategic planning itself (Peters and Waterman 1982; Peters 1992a; Mintzberg 1994a).

INDIVIDUAL GENIUS OR ORGANIZATIONAL CAPABILITY?

In spite of its importance, we still have much to learn about how to develop the capacity for innovation in organizational settings, and about how to leverage it in pursuit of sustainable competitive advantage. Is the capacity for innovation and entrepreneurship mainly a personal attribute, or is it primarily an organizational process? Do companies that wish to build sustainable competitive advantage on entrepreneurial capability have to rely mainly on their ability to recruit and retain a core of key individuals of rare talent and inspiration? These questions remain central in the literature on innovation.

There have been many attempts to isolate the characteristics that distinguish innovative or entrepreneurial people from the rest of the population, based on the conviction that these rare and inspired individuals are born and not made. For example, John G. Burch provides the following profile:

> Although entrepreneurs cannot be completely defined, certain characteristics and tendencies can be used to paint their profile. They want to achieve, are willing to work hard, able to nurture, and disposed to accept responsibility. Oriented towards reward they are optimists, with an inclination towards excellence, a knack for organization, and a desire to make a profit. They seek independence, wealth, opportunity, innovation, and venture, accept risk, and rely on intuition.
>
> (Burch 1986: 16)

Such profiles, and the personality trait approach in general, are 'not especially effective in identifying prospective entrepreneurs', according to Morris and Trotter (1990: 132), or in clearly discriminating a distinct entrepreneurial personality type. Many of these characteristics are widely distributed among people who show very little in the way of innovative or entrepreneurial tendencies. Furthermore, the evidence remains equivocal at best even in the case of those attributes, such as propensity to seek risk, that could have predictive value. It is commonly believed that entrepreneurs are high in propensity for risk-taking. Peter Drucker (1985) is prominent among those who dispute this belief. He is also to the fore in questioning the existence of a distinct entrepreneurial personality, a scepticism shared by successful entrepreneurs of his acquaintance. While entrepreneurs accept risk in their ventures, they try to minimize it. For Drucker, entrepreneurship is a process that can be systematized and widely practised. According to him, 'innovation is organized, systematic, rational work' in which 'everyone who can face up to decision making can learn to be an entrepreneur and to behave entrepreneurially' (Drucker 1985: 40, 65). Companies with long track records of innovation, like 3M and Proctor & Gamble, are cited as examples of the successful systematization of entrepreneurship, independent of the vagaries of the entrepreneurial personality.

Clearly there is much about innovation and entrepreneurship

that can be systematized. Siemens and Westinghouse are further examples of companies whose innovative capacity has survived well beyond the tenures of the founding entrepreneurs. Furthermore, the recent passing of such towering figures as Soichiro Honda (1907–1991) and Sam Walton (1918–1992) of Wal-Mart had very little impact on the valuation of their companies. This was evidence of the degree to which the market at the time believed that the capacity of both of these companies for innovation and enterprise had been successfully institutionalized. However, it is unlikely that the same would yet hold true today in the case of, say, Bill Gates and Microsoft. The role of the rare individual and the unique talent still has a central significance in any consideration of innovation and entrepreneurship, and of the firm-specific competitive advantages associated with them. Moreover, the firm-specific advantages accruing from the unique talents of key individuals are not confined to the leadership alone. As Schneiderman (1991: 55), the former vice-president of research and development at Monsanto, has argued, 'outstanding researchers are a rare breed' and 'most seminal discoveries are made by a handful of outstanding researchers'. The firm-specific advantages associated with innovation and entrepreneurship are, it seems, firmly rooted in both individual talents and systematic organizational capabilities.

THE 'SILVER BULLET' OR THE 'THOUSAND FLOWERS'?

To understand more fully the strategic potency of innovation, we must go beyond the question of whether it is primarily idiosyncratic or systemic in nature and examine the dynamics of the process itself, and how they affect both company prospects and industry structures.

Innovation is most often associated with technology, and the process of innovation with the process of technological change. It is now generally recognized that truly radical and frame-breaking technological innovations in any industry are rare (Drucker 1985; Tushman and Anderson 1986; Utterback 1994). The prevalent pattern in most industries is one of long periods of evolutionary or continuous incremental technological development punctuated by rare episodes of discontinuous or radical innovation. Tushman and Anderson (1986), for example, found a total of just eight discontinuous changes over the combined 190-year history of the US cement, airline and minicomputer industries. There was just one such radical change in the 200-year history of the Irish distilling industry (Leavy and Wilson 1994). However, such frame-breaking changes can be 'at once the creators and destroyers of industries and corporations', whenever they do occur (Utterback 1994: xiv). Moreover, they 'tend to be driven by individual genius', as in the cases of Carlson and Xerography or Pilkington and float glass, and this makes them nearly impossible to predict and anticipate (Tushman and Anderson 1986: 440). It will always, it seems, be difficult to build strategic intent (Hamel and Prahalad 1989) upon the deliberate pursuit of such innovations within any given company, and it will be difficult to defend against them arising elsewhere.

Product and process innovation, and the dominant design

Not all that is strategically important about the innovation process is as difficult to predict or anticipate as technological break-through. We know from recent studies of the dynamics of the process (Utterback and Abernathy 1975; Tushman and Anderson 1986; Utterback 1994) that technological trajectories in many industries, particularly those involving assembled products like the automobile, consumer electronics and office machines industries, follow a fairly general pattern over time. We also know that product and process innovation are related in predictable ways. Many new industries begin with a period of technological ferment when the rate of product innovation is at its peak. The opportunities offered by the birth of the new industry attract a large and diverse number of players, each hoping that its particular version of the new product will find most favour with the emerging market. What happens at this early stage, when viewed at the level of industrial dynamics, is that scores of separate independent experiments are being carried out to find the version of the product that will ultimately come to enjoy the highest level of consumer acceptance. This initial phase is followed by the emergence of a dominant design, as the industry standard. It is only after the emergence of the dominant design that the future trajectory of the technology becomes predictable enough for the leading firms to begin to make commitments to process improvement, and to concentrate on the types of standardization and specialization that lead to scale economies and the minimization of costs. The emergence of the dominant design sees the rules of the competitive game change to process innovation and incremental product development. It brings with it a drastic reduction in the number of viable players, as those with the product designs least compatible with the dominant one get selected out. The emergence of the internal combustion engine in the automobile industry and the sealed refrigeration unit in home appliances are just two examples of this common pattern.

The rewards that can come from truly radical innovations or technological 'silver bullets' can be great, as the early histories of companies such as Xerox and Polaroid would attest. However, the costs and risks associated with such innovations are usually high, and a company can see its entire investment come to nought if it fails to establish its new product as industry standard. This risk is particularly great if there are resourceful competitors in the race, or even in the wings. There are many factors that eventually lead to one or another version of an innovation becoming accepted as industry standard. Technical superiority is not always decisive. The success of Matsushita over Sony in the battle that established VHS rather than Betamax as industry standard in video-recorder technology is one of the best-known examples.

Creative imitation and collective entrepreneurship

Many innovating firms also often lose out to imitators, and fail to obtain the significant economic benefits that their creative activities might seem to merit. The question of which company benefits most from any radical innovation often turns on the factors of the technology protection regime operating in the industry, and on the importance of complementary assets. As Teece (1986: 287) has pointed out, 'many patents can be invented around at modest costs', and are 'especially ineffective at protecting process innovations'. Furthermore, the widespread practice of reverse engineering ensures that few 'trade secrets' can be adequately protected, once the product is on the market. In many industries, resourceful imitators can have their own modifications of the basic design, or applications of the new technology, on the market before the dominant design has emerged. The existence of complementary assets, like an established brand name or company-owned service network, can prove decisive in determining whether the imitator's design will ultimately become the dominant one at the expense of the innovator. There are many examples of innovators that have lost out in this way, like EMI in scanners, Xerox in office computers, and DeHavilland in jet aircraft. Among the best-known examples of winning imitators are Seiko in wristwatches and Texas Instruments in pocket calculators.

The Utterback and Abernathy model of innovation dynamics shows that once the dominant design emerges, the commercial rules of the game change. Speed to market with product enhancements and innovation to make the process more efficient become the critical drivers of ongoing competitiveness. Proficiency in these areas depends more on development engineering capability, and on the nature of the management process, than it does on rare and fundamental technical skills. It depends on creativity and innovation of a different kind than that which produces the technological 'silver bullet' or radical breakthrough, but one that is often more important in the long run. The success of many Japanese companies, in securing market leadership in industries that were initially founded on Western invention, was based on what we are now coming to recognize as a strategy of 'creative imitation' (Drucker 1985; Rosenberg and Steinmueller 1988; Bolton 1993a). The essence of creative imitation might be captured in the notion of imitation in fundamental technology combined with innovation in its full development and commercialization. Matsushita, for example, reached its position as the world's largest manufacturer of electrical appliances by perfecting a strategy of creative imitation, with apologies to no one. One of its most senior American executives has described the company's strategy in the following way:

> If you watch where Matsushita puts its resources, its success through followership comes as no surprise. They have 23 production research laboratories equipped with the latest technology available. Their concept of research and development is to analyze competing products and figure out how to do better.
>
> (Pascale and Athos 1981: 31)

The success of creative imitators, like Matsushita, has helped to direct renewed attention in the West to long-neglected elements of the innovative process, and their links with competitiveness and economic performance. As Rosenberg and Steinmueller (1988) have pointed out, Western thinking about the innovation process has tended to focus excessively on the activities of the upstream inventor or scientist, rather than the downstream engineer. The dominant view of the innovative process 'is still overly Schumpeterian, in its preoccupation with discontinuities and creative destruction, and its neglect of the cumulative power of numerous small, incremental changes' (p. 230). In fact, as Stata (1989) and others have pointed out, the rise of Japan as an economic power is unique in modern commercial history in being rooted not in the foundation of new industries through radical technological innovation but in the domination of existing industries based on management innovation. Two key features of the Japanese approach have been the belief in the cumulative impact of numerous small ideas in pursuit of improvements in product and process, what Kanter (1988) and others have referred to as the 'thousand flowers' approach to innovation, and a superior ability to manage the innovation process in a more timely, integrative and collective way than has been the tradition in most Western companies. In fact some prominent economic commentators, like Robert Reich (1987), now believe that technological trajectories have become, if anything, more evolutionary in many industries, from consumer electronics and automobiles to basic materials like steel and ceramics. The collective capacity of organizations to push a basic technology in new directions, continuously refining it into a stream of new products, which can in turn spawn further evolutionary technological trajectories, is becoming more and more the primary engine of wealth creation in the modern economy. In short, the implication is that Western society must learn to 'honour [its] teams more' and its 'aggressive leaders and maverick geniuses less', if it is 'to compete effectively in today's world' (Reich 1987: 78).

After a slow start it is now clear that many Western companies have begun to absorb the lessons of the Japanese approach to innovation in industries from automobiles to office machines. In some businesses like mass retailing, where Schumpeterian discontinuities are least likely to be influential, many leading Western companies, like Marks & Spencer and Wal-Mart Stores, have long since discovered for themselves the cumulative impact of the 'thousand flowers' approach to innovation and competitiveness, and have been using it proficiently for much of their existence (Leavy 1991a). The impact of this approach on many industries seems to support Drucker's argument that an organization's capacity for innovation is primarily rooted in its management process rather than in its possession of rare talent (Drucker 1985). However, we should continue to recognize that rare talent and technological breakthroughs are still capable of lifting existing industries on to new planes of development. As more and more competitors become proficient at downstream product development and process improvement, the power of more radical innovations in both product and process design may become a more compelling source of competitive advantage than it has been in recent times. Sooner or later the underlying economics may once again have to favour first movers, and technological breakthroughs, in the overall dynamics of economic development, or there will be no movement. What does a creative imitator do when it catches up with the industry leader and wants to maintain its economic performance? It may have to turn to more radical innovation, as Komatsu found, in its rivalry with Caterpillar, in the earth-moving equipment industry.

THE ESTABLISHED ORGANIZATION AND RADICAL INNOVATION

Time and again the business literature has shown that most innovation, particularly of the more radical kind, tends to come from outside existing industries and established organizations (Kanter 1983; Drucker 1985; Peters 1990; Utterback 1994; Bower and Christensen 1995). As Peters and Waterman (1982: 200) noted, 'the most discouraging fact of big corporate life is the loss of what got them big in the first place: innovation'. From Bic in writing instruments to CNN in television broadcasting, the pattern has been repeated over and over again. Radical innovations with revolutionary implications for the future structure of whole industries are often introduced by new and relatively small invaders. Why do established firms seem to be comparatively poor at radical innovation?

Is the established organization motivated to innovate?

Schumpeter's now classic theory of economic development still provides the most widely used framework for the economic analysis of innovation (Schumpeter 1934). To students of the strategy process his ideas contain a seeming paradox. In conditions of perfect competition, the whole economic system tends towards equilibrium and efficiency. However, the process of economic growth and development involves propelling the economy from one level of equilibrium to a higher level. This cannot be done in a gradual incremental fashion. It seems to require discontinuous change, or creative destruction of the existing equilibrium. The resources required for creative destruction can only be generated through market imperfection and surplus profit. These conditions of partial market failure favour the emergence of the larger organization in any industry, and fairly high levels of industry concentration (Williamson 1975). The presence of large organizations that are capable of earning above average returns seems to be an essential requirement for radical innovation. Yet, as noted earlier, the empirical evidence suggests that radical innovation tends to come from outside these organizations. One explanation for this apparent paradox is that original research carried out within many large, resourceful companies often subsequently leaks out because these organizations are unwilling or unable to commercialize it. Data General, for example, was founded by disillusioned engineers from Digital Equipment Corporation, whose original ideas had failed to win the support of their former employer (Kidder 1981). Apple Computers successfully commercialized many basic innovations that were developed, but underexploited, by Xerox Corporation (Scully 1987).

We can also draw some explanation for the failure of established firms to generate and commercialize technological breakthroughs from the frameworks of Porter (1980), and Utterback and Abernathy (Utterback and Abernathy 1975; Utterback 1994). Discontinuous technological change appears in Porter's framework for industry analysis mainly in the form of the threat of substitute products. Substitute products based on radically different product technology or raw materials are a force for creative destruction. They threaten to destabilize totally the existing industry equilibrium, not only by hastening the onset of the decline phase in the existing product life cycle, but also by potentially opening up the industry to powerful new entrants with existing economies of scale, scope and experience based on the new technology or materials in question. The transformation of the global wristwatch industry, which flowed from the introduction of electronic quartz crystal technology, is one of the classic examples. Established market leaders, therefore, often have very mixed feelings about the promotion of radical innovations that are likely to make their existing products obsolete and destabilize their industries. For reasons such as these, it appears that high performing firms or industry leaders, as Michele Kremen Bolton's research has indicated, tend to 'develop incremental rather than radical innovations, and defend current positions rather than aggressively seeking new opportunities' (Bolton 1993b: 60–1). Organizations with a large performance gap between their aspirations and resources are often the most creative – they have to be to realize their ambitions, as Hamel and Prahalad (1989) point out. It is perhaps little wonder then that 'firms that ride an innovation to the heights of industrial leadership more often than not fail to shift to newer technologies' (Utterback 1994: 162), and that industrial leadership 'changes hands in about seven out of ten cases when discontinuities strike' (Foster 1986: 116).

Further explanation for the reluctance of established firms to pursue and promote radical innovation is provided by the institutionalist literature. As new ventures grow into established firms the once radical innovation becomes institutionalized into the firm's activities, operating norms and routines (Zucker 1987). This stabilizing process is part of what is necessary to reap the maximum economic benefits from the innovation over the full course of the product life cycle. As time progresses, the established industry leader makes major specialized investments in plant, equipment and human skills that are linked to the technology of the dominant design. The organization also develops strong emotional commitments to the technology that was the primary foundation of its current success. At industry level also, the onset of the dominant design and equilibrium leads to the emergence of certain norms and recipes that tend to stabilize the rules of the game (Grinyer and Spender 1979). These conventional wisdoms have time and again proved to be serious blind-spots for current participants. The skiing industry in the early 1950s, for example, 'knew' that skis had to be made of wood, not metal; the writing instruments industry in the 1960s 'knew' that you could not successfully market a branded low-price disposable ball-point; and the mass retailing industry in the 1970s 'knew' that discount stores could not be made to operate commercially outside metropolitan areas with populations of at least 100,000. New entrants like Howard Head, Marcel Bich and Sam Walton proved them wrong, and greatly enriched themselves in the process. Furthermore, had these innovations, or challenges to the conventional wisdom, come from within the industry they would have been more quickly spotted and imitated. The process of institutionalization at industry level makes the incumbents particularly insensitive to the outside threats. Head, Bich and Walton all had the advantage of being able to 'fly under the industry's radar' for long enough to establish very secure bridgeheads before any serious response was mounted.

Is the established organization able to innovate?

We have reviewed above some of the main reasons why established firms might seem reluctant to pursue and promote radical innovation. However, there are many who question not just the motivation of such organizations to innovate but also their basic capability do so. Can the established firm really innovate? There are two related questions here. First, can the established firm successfully manage the process that generates creative and innovative solutions to product-market opportunities in the first instance? Second, can such firms manage the kind of internal renewal and transformation that are typically required to give most such radical innovations full effect? The first question we shall deal with below; the second will be the main focus of a later chapter.

Many writers have attempted to isolate the essential characteristics of the innovation process (Quinn 1979, 1985; Kanter 1988; Peters 1990, 1991). Most now agree that the innovation process – in whatever organizational context, large or small – is essentially a probabilistic one. Success is never guaranteed. No matter how much we try to systematize it, the process remains at root one of 'controlled chaos' (Quinn 1985). As Peters (1990: 17) has argued 'innovation, in the end and no matter how well thought out, is a numbers game'. Success requires 'requisite variety' or 'kaleidoscopic' diversity in idea generation (Burgleman 1983a; Kanter 1988). It also requires multiple competing approaches to improve the odds for success substantially. It further requires a degree of personal or small group fanaticism to persist in the initial period of high risk, high frustration and low reward. Even the most spectacular innovations are rarely obvious 'biggies' at the beginning (Drucker 1985; Peters 1990). Successful innovation seems to require a fair degree of personal and financial slack to provide sufficient scope for experimentation (Quinn 1985; Kanter 1988; Peters 1990). Finally, it seems to benefit from the closest possible link between the marketplace and technology, and a context that can tolerate and learn from failure. We see all these characteristics of innovation at work in the process of new business creation throughout the wider economic environment. Can such an inherently diverse and probabilistic process be successfully institutionalized within a single organization?

It is now widely recognized that there are substantial potential barriers to the successful institutionalization of such a process with an established corporate hierarchy. Quinn (1985) has identified the most notable and common of these as top management conservatism and isolation from the innovative process, intolerance for fanatics and 'non-conformist' talent, short time horizons for expecting payback, excessive rationalization and routinization of the process, excessive bureaucracy and inappropriate rewards. Others have identified similar obstacles (Sinetar 1985; Morris and Trotter 1990).

Sinetar (1985) has made a very interesting distinction between two types of creative entrepreneurs, the activist and the creative thinker. The activist is 'a doer' with 'an innate understanding of what it takes to run, expand, reconceptualize or create a business' (p. 57). Intuitive activists, like Victor Kiam of Remington, Akio Morita of Sony or Richard Branson of Virgin, are 'natural dance partners' to business and organizational life (p. 57). It is the second type, the creative thinker, whom organizational life typically finds difficult to accommodate. These are the non-conformist inventive types, who typically like to immerse themselves in technical and scientific challenges. They often do it for the sheer intellectual pleasure of the chase, and in any role their habits tend to 'contradict organizational expectations and mores' (p. 58). The reward and control systems in most established organizations 'are designed to minimize surprise' (Quinn 1985: 77), yet in research 'surprises are the name of the game' (Schneiderman 1991: 54). Those whose inventions or commercial ideas are pivotal in making their companies very rich seldom see this reflected in their own pay or conditions. In the case of many such creative scientists and engineers, the most valued reward is the recognition that their inventiveness earns them in the eyes of their professional peers. Their reputations in their fields are often independent of their standings within their companies. Opportunities to publish and to present to professional meetings may be more important to them than their position on the organizational chart, an orientation that many company executives tend to view as idiosyncratic 'self-indulgence' (Schneiderman 1991: 54).

Institutionalizing innovation in the established firm is clearly not easy. However, there are many notable examples of long-established firms, like 3M, Honda and ABB, that have managed to preserve their capacity for innovation as they have grown (Peters and Waterman 1982; Kanter 1983; Quinn 1985; Stevenson and Jarillo 1986). Most have typically done this by being able to depart from the traditional bureaucratic model, in a number of ways that can accommodate some of the inherent messiness of the innovation process and its probabilistic nature (see Morris and Trotter 1990 and Mitsch 1992 for specific examples). To begin with, such organizations usually try to establish a general organizational climate that clearly emphasizes the importance of innovation. At Honda, for example, it has long been the tradition that the route to the leadership of the company has been through the R&D activity. Such organizations often encourage the pursuit of multiple competing approaches that culminate in development shoot-outs. This helps to generate the kind of diversity required for success, and to bring the motivating effects of the 'technical chase' in-house. These organizations often encourage the formation of informal garage-type operations, where small teams of fanatics can get together with seed capital and few bureaucratic constraints during the early stages of the innovation process. Such companies usually try to create an internal climate that enables enterprising champions to assemble the political support and resources needed to steer new initiatives over the many institutional hurdles that the established organization presents (Maidique 1980; Kanter 1982). In the larger organization the crucial champion is often the middle manager who assumes the role of 'business innovator' (Maidique 1980) or 'intuitive activist' (Sinetar 1985), rather than the technical originator. In such a context, the credibility, commitment and clout of this individual can often be the decisive factor in getting an innovation through to full commercialization (Bower 1970; Burgleman 1983a).

In their classic study of innovation, Burns and Stalker (1966) conceptualized two ideal types of organization: the free-flowing organic type, which was best suited to innovation and change, and the mechanistic type, best suited to stability and efficiency. Many of the established organizations dedicated to preserving their capacity to innovate, try to incorporate some elements of the free-flowing approach without losing the main efficiency benefits of the more formalized structure. This always creates a dynamic tension within the organization that is difficult to manage, and is one of the many delicate balancing acts at the heart of modern strategic management. Even Drucker (1985: 171), the most prominent advocate of the view that innovation is primarily a systemic organizational process, has acknowledged that 'it takes special effort for the existing business to become entrepreneurial and innovative'. He believes that the new internal venturing activity has to be organized separately from existing operations. Trying to combine the best of both forms of operation within the one organization remains a major challenge (Bower and Christensen 1995).

Entrepreneurial organizations typically face two types of structural problems as they develop. One is how to preserve their capacity for innovation, which has been the main theme of this chapter. The other is managing the transition from a free-flowing start-up operation to a professionally managed company, if they are not to come apart at the seams as they grow. Ironically, the founding entrepreneur often comes to present the most formidable obstacle in both cases. Steve Jobs of Apple, Soichiro Honda and Clive Sinclair are among the many that have had difficulties with the management of transition. Honda solved it through his business partnership with Takeo Fujisawa, a man with complementary organizational skills. Steve Jobs had similar hopes for his relationship with John Sculley, but it didn't work out. Other entrepreneurs, like Phil Knight of Nike, have tried to adapt their operating styles as their enterprises have grown, but have seldom found it easy. The founding entrepreneur is often also the greatest impediment to the successful institutionalization of free-flowing entrepreneurial activity within the established firm, because of an inability or unwillingness to devolve the entrepreneurial mantle to others, whether they be venture groups, 'skunk works' or whatever (Stevenson and Jarillo 1986). Since the 'entrepreneur' has long enjoyed heroic status in Western management culture, it is only relatively recently that the darker side of entrepreneurship is being more closely examined (Osborne 1991), and the true importance of the gifted individual in the process of innovation and economic development is being more critically assessed (Kaplan 1987; Reich 1987).

Overall, the management of the free-flowing organic and the efficient mechanistic structures and processes within the same organization is difficult. Some authors have suggested that organizations need to develop the capacity to cycle between the two types (Slevin and Covin 1990), but this is just as problematic as trying to manage both simultaneously. The transformations involved, as we shall see in a later chapter, are likely to be at least as challenging. In sum, it would appear that the capacity to innovate can be institutionalized to a significant degree in established companies. However, the recent traumas of companies like IBM and Digital in the computer industry, with track records as innovative organizations extending over thirty years or more, suggests that this capacity is always limited. 'No tree grows to the sky', as Nuala Beck (1992: 91–2) has recently reminded us, 'and hard as it is to accept' it may well be that in this, as in other aspects of organizational life, 'nothing goes on forever, even for the brightest and the best'. Radical innovation will continue to involve a process of decay and renewal, not only within organizations but also at industry level, and most organizations will find it very difficult and challenging to survive this process intact over the longer term.

SUMMARY

In this chapter we examined a number of important aspects of the innovation process and their links with competitiveness and economic performance. Among the major themes that still actively engage the field of strategic management is the question of whether innovative capacity is mainly rooted in individual human resources or in organizational processes. We then examined some aspects of the dynamics of the innovation process at industry level, and the changing roles of product and process innovation in the determination of competitiveness at different stages of the product cycle. We highlighted the growing interest in collective entrepreneurship and creative imitation, and explored these two important aspects of the strategic potency of innovation, which were brought to the fore by the success of Japanese companies in many internationalizing industries over the last two decades. Finally we explored some of the reasons why established companies seem to be comparatively sluggish and poor at innovation, and why it remains the case that radical innovation still tends to happen outside existing industries and their leading incumbents.

The growing interest in collective entrepreneurship, and in innovation as an organization-wide process of continuous improvement and knowledge generation, leads naturally to a closely related interest in how individuals and collectives learn in organizational settings, and how organizational learning is linked to competitiveness. This will be the major focus of the next chapter.

Chapter 3

Learning

In truth, we had no strategy other than the idea of seeing if we could sell something in the United States. It was a new frontier, a new challenge, and it fit the 'success against all odds' culture that Mr Honda had cultivated.

Kihachiro Kawashima, Honda Corporation

Richard Pascale's case history of Honda's successful penetration of the US motorcycle industry, from which the opening quotation is sourced (Pascale 1984: 54), is often cited as one of the most powerful illustrations of the process view of strategy making. It is also frequently cited as one of the classic illustrations of the 'strategy as learning' notion, which has since grown to become one of the most powerful themes in current strategy literature (Mintzberg 1987, 1990). Honda's successful entry into the US market was ultimately based more on the ability of the company to experiment, adapt and learn during the entry process than on any prior strategic insight or competitive master plan. In the context of the new economy, the information age and the growth of knowledge-intensive industries, more and more commentators are coming to agree with the view recently expressed by Ray Stata of Analog Devices, that 'the rate at which individuals and organizations learn may become the only sustainable source of competitive advantage' (Stata 1989: 64).

In this chapter, the role that the concept of learning has played historically in the strategy field is reviewed, and its potential as a model for the strategy process itself is examined. The pervasiveness of the notion of collective learning, as the key process underpinning the recent core competencies (Prahalad and Hamel 1990), core capabilities (Stalk *et al.* 1992), and core activities (Quinn *et al.* 1990a) approaches to building competitiveness, is then highlighted and discussed. The chapter then goes on to analyse the links between learning and innovation, and between individual and organizational learning. It ends with a discussion of some of the issues and debates linking learning with competitiveness, which remain challenging and unresolved.

THE LEARNING CONCEPT IN STRATEGY – A HISTORICAL PERSPECTIVE

Learning as a source of competitive advantage – economies of experience

The association of learning with strategy and competitive advantage has a long history. During the 1960s the Boston Consulting Group (BCG), under the leadership of Bruce Henderson, popularized the concept of the experience curve as a powerful analytical tool in the strategy formulation process. While the notion of 'economies of experience' had already been around in the economics literature for some time (Galbraith 1956: 47), Henderson and his group were able to quantify the effect (Henderson 1973). They demonstrated that in many industries unit costs could be seen to decrease with cumulative volume in a predictable and exponential fashion. In the then newly emerging semiconductor industry, for example, the price per unit fell from $25 to $1 as the industry's cumulative volume grew from 2 million to 2 billion units over the 1964–72 period. Henderson believed that market leaders (with the highest cumulative volumes) enjoyed a significant cost advantage because of the experience effect. This cost advantage offered many potential strategic benefits. Experience-based pricing was a very effective way for early movers like Bic in disposable ball-point pens to maintain market leadership and deter late entrants. The experience effect was assumed to be the primary advantage enjoyed by stars and cash-cows in the well-known BCG growth-share business portfolio matrix. The advantage was assumed to be sustainable, if market leadership could be maintained.

Experienced-based strategies have delivered mixed results over the years. There are many examples of companies that have achieved sustained economic success with this type of approach, including Lincoln Electric in arc welding, Bausch & Lomb in contact lenses, and Texas Instruments in calculators. On the other hand, the business literature is also full of stories of experience-based strategies that either failed to live up to initial expectations, like Du Pont in the titanium industry, or were initially successful but ultimately disastrous, like Ford's Model T. Ford created the mass market for automobiles, through its aggressive focus on cost reduction using economies of scale and experience. However, when General Motors under Alfred Sloan changed the rules of the game, by being able to combine scale and experience economies at component level with variety at product level, Ford found it difficult to respond, and ultimately lost its market leadership.

Building strategy on the experience effect – the risks

While experience-based strategies can be very potent sources of sustainable competitive advantage, it has long been recognized that the conditions under which such strategies tend to succeed or fail need to be fully understood (Ghemawat 1985). To begin with, the strength of the potential experience effect has been found to vary from industry to industry, ranging from 40 per cent (unit costs declining by 40 per cent with every doubling of cumulative volume) to practically zero, with a 15 per cent effect being most typical. Some companies, like Monsanto in acrylonitrile manu-facturing, suffered losses as a result of overestimating the experience effect, because the anticipated cost advantages just never materialized. Furthermore, the impact of the effect tends to vary over the product life cycle, being strongest at the beginning when the rate of increase in unit volumes is at its highest.

The presence of a strong experience effect is one of the factors that can often favour an imitative or second-mover strategy, where the initial costs of the innovation are high and the protection regime for the innovation is relatively weak. In these circum-stances, an imitator with lower entry investment may be more willing than the innovator to follow an experience-curve pricing strategy, in the aggressive pursuit of market leadership with its self-sustaining cost advantage. Furthermore, where the innovator is small, it often lacks the resources needed to invest in a successful experience-based strategy, which usually requires pre-emptive 'lumpy' investments in manufacturing and marketing scale and scope to be fully effective (Chandler 1990). Moreover, there are risks in trying to pursue an aggressive experience-curve strategy in advance of the emergence of the dominant design. The sought-after cost advantages may end up being based on the wrong technology, and ultimately prove worthless. Finally, the highly focused pursuit of economies of experience can leave a company in a very vulnerable position, when the threat of substitute products is high, and new players, with price-performance advantages based on a totally different experience curve, are able to enter the market easily.

Learning as a model of the strategy process

In addition to its long-standing association with the experience effect, the concept of learning has for some time now been emerging within the field in an even more fundamental way, as a model for the strategy process itself.

Strategy, when the field first emerged in the 1960s, was conceptualized primarily as a planning process. The concept of strategy as planning has since had a chequered history, as we saw in Chapter 2. Its critics argue that it has risen and fallen in this time (Mintzberg 1994a). Its more ardent supporters acknowledge that it has at least transmuted into the more flexible and responsive notion of strategic management (Ansoff 1994). Most would agree that our understanding of strategy has now moved well beyond the early planning models to encompass a more dynamic and complex view of the process. The notion of strategy as a learning process is continuing to gain currency, even among those with a strong practical background in the planning paradigm. At Royal Dutch Shell, for example, they now think of planning as learning, and corporate planning as institutional learning (de Geus 1988).

The early roots of the learning model of the strategy process can be traced back to Quinn and Mintzberg. Quinn's model of strategy as a learning process of logical incrementalism remains one of the most influential in the field (Quinn 1978). What became clear to him, and to many others in the late 1970s, was that the carefully designed planning systems of major corporations were not performing well. He found that many such companies did appear to have cohesive strategies, but that these strategies 'seemed to come from someplace other than the formal planning process' (Quinn 1989: 55). He believed that the incremental way in which he found strategy developed in companies like Pilkington Glass, General Foods and Xerox had a logic, based on a learning approach, that other companies should follow. He argued that companies should generally 'proceed flexibly and experimentally from broad concepts towards specific commitments', because they were trying to deal with the 'unknowable' rather than the 'uncertain', such as unpredictable precipitating events like oil crises, frame-breaking innovations, and forces of such great number, strength and combinatory powers (Quinn 1989: 55).

It was Mintzberg (1978) who first made the insightful distinction between strategy formulation and strategy formation, though the notion of strategy as an emergent as well as deliberate process had already been around for some time (Bower 1970; Allison 1971). More recently Mintzberg (1987) has put forward a crafting view of the strategy process, which he argues is not only a more accurate representation of how strategy is made than the formal planning view but also a more useful prescriptive guide. In Mintzberg's metaphor, strategists are craftsmen that 'sit between a past of corporate capabilities and a future of market opportunities', and use their intimate knowledge of the materials at hand to mould a strategy (p. 66). The roles of learning and tacit knowledge are central to this metaphor, which combines technology with imagination, and self-conscious analytical processes with a more tacit experiential sense of things. In Mintzberg's view 'all strategy making walks on two feet, one deliberate and one emergent' (p. 69). The emergent dimension fosters learning, while the deliberate dimension fosters control.

The concept of learning, in short, is now attracting increasing interest in the strategy field, because of its conceptual as well as its practical potential. As Mark Dodgson has pointed out, the concept of learning is attractive because (i) it has 'broad analytical value', which is reflected in the ever-widening range of disciplines using it; (ii) it is essentially 'dynamic' in nature, and unlike the concepts of planning or decision making, it emphasizes the continually changing nature of organizations; and (iii) it is inherently 'integrative' and capable of unifying individual, organizational, and sectoral levels of analysis (Dodgson 1993: 376).

MODERN COMPETITIVE ANALYSIS AND THE LEARNING PROCESS

Modern competitive analysis is one of the many areas where the notion of learning is becoming more central and pervasive. With industries growing more volatile, and product life cycles short-ening, the main focus in the search for sustainable competitive advantage has shifted away from industry analysis and market positioning to internal capabilities. This shift is reflected in the renewed interest being taken in the economic growth theories of Edith Penrose (1959). It is also reflected in the growing influence of the resource-based view of the firm in the strategy field (Wernerfelt 1984; Conner 1991), with its focus on the identification and analysis of 'firm-specific advantages', which are rooted in a company's 'portfolio of differential core skills and routines, coherence across skills and unique proprietary know-how' (Mahoney and Pandian 1992: 369). The current interest in core competencies, activities, and capabilities, as the foundations for competitiveness in the new economy, is a reflection of this growing influence. The notion of learning is central in all these emerging perspectives, as we shall see below.

Core competencies

Prahalad and Hamel (1990) were among the first to argue that in today's economic environment market position is no longer a reliable indicator of competitive strength. World manufacturing share of core components, which embody key technologies with diverse applications, is often a better indicator of where the real economies of scale, scope and experience, and the difficult-to-imitate firm-specific advantages, are to be found. Honda, Philips, Canon, Intel and Sony are all examples of companies whose economic influence across a diverse range of industries is more accurately discernible in global manufacturing share of key components and technologies, rather than market share in end products. Honda competes across a variety of sectors, including automobiles and outdoor power equipment, and is market leader in only one: motorcycles. Yet, it is highly competitive in all of them, owing in large measure to its position as the world's leading manufacturer of small engines and power trains, the key components of all motorized equipment. These core products, or key components, are the tradable parts of the more fundamental drivers of competitiveness – the core competencies of the companies involved. Such strategic competencies are more than just technologies, and reflect 'collective learning' in how to 'coordinate diverse production skills and integrate multiple streams of technologies' (Prahalad and Hamel 1990: 82). It is the embeddedness of these competencies within the social fabric and processes of the organization that makes them so difficult to imitate. Firms that build their futures on the basis of carefully selected competencies, rather than markets, focus the strategy process on the issue of how best to match depth in firm-specific learning with breadth in its commercial application, since 'few companies are likely to build world leadership in more than five or six fundamental competencies' (p. 84).

Activity-based strategy and core capabilities

Similar perspectives on the changing nature of competition, and the role of learning, have been emerging recently in the services area. New information-based technologies, combined in some cases with deregulation, are revolutionizing service industries, from banking and consultancy to restaurants and retailing. According to Quinn *et al.* (1990b: 60), 'smart strategists no longer analyze market shares' to determine competitiveness in the service sector either, but closely examine their value chains to identify 'those core service activities where their company has or can develop unique capabilities'. Developing economies of scale, scope and experience in these critical activities, which are leverageable across a diverse range of marketable services, becomes the primary concern, and activity share rather than market share becomes the primary indicator of economic influence. Super-Valu in retailing and Arthur Andersen in consulting are among the many companies now pursuing such activity-focused strategies. Non-leverageable activities in the value chain, like facility maintenance or payroll processing, can in many cases be better contracted out to specialists, with economies of scale, scope and experience in these particular areas which no non-specialist can match. Once again the notion of learning is very central to this activity-focused approach to competitiveness in services. According to Quinn *et al.* (1990), 'a maintainable advantage usually derives from outstanding depth in selected human skills, logistics capabilities, knowledge bases, or other service strengths that competitors cannot reproduce and that lead to demonstrable value for the customer' (p. 60).

Some see the future key to competitiveness lying not so much in what a company does as how it does it. According to this perspective, the development of exceptional cross-functional process capabilities should be the main strategic concern (Stalk 1988; Stalk *et al.* 1992; Hammer 1990; Hammer and Champy 1993). In today's environment, as Stalk *et al.* (1992: 62) see it, the 'essence of strategy is *not* the structure of a company's products and markets' but 'the dynamics of its behaviour', and competition is now a 'war of movement' rather than position. Companies like Sony, Benetton and Federal Express have consistently outper-formed larger-scale competitors by being more responsive, flexible and efficient in their management of key business processes, such as product development and operational logistics. Through these exceptional process capabilities, they have been more effective in leveraging the creativity and efficiency of their employees in key overhead areas where, as Drucker (1991) points out, the big productivity gains in the future are most likely to be found. Among the typical examples highlighted by Stalk (1988), was the case of a Japanese auto-components manufacturer which was able to outperform its US counterpart in productivity and product variety, despite having only one third of the volume. The explanation was that its overhead employees were over fifty times more productive, not because they were better people but because they used better processes. For Stalk and his colleagues (1992), the key, firm-specific, resource-based advantage is rooted not only in core competencies or activities but, more importantly, in compe-tency-spanning and process-linking capabilities, like Wal-Mart's in logistics or Honda's in new product 'realization'. It is a view of strategy that sees business processes as the fundamental building blocks, and the linking of these processes into difficult-to-imitate core capabilities as the key to sustainable competitive advantage. Again, the concept of learning is very much to the fore.

In sum, while the core competencies, activities and capabilities approaches have somewhat different perspectives, they share a number of key elements. All emphasize the more dynamic nature of strategy in the modern economic environment, and the need to look beyond product-market positioning in the analysis of competitiveness. All of them emphasize the importance of concentrating on a few critical internal sources of competitive advantage, which are capable of being leveraged across a wide range of product-market opportunities. All of them embrace the notion of resource-based advantages that appreciate, rather than depreciate, with use over time, and that have learning and its fruits as the keys to this appreciation. Finally, all of these sources of advantage are seen as key corporate-level resources that can be leveraged to enhance business-level competitiveness, often with the timely and efficient transfer of learning across the different business units as the main value-adding process.

LEARNING AND INNOVATION

One of the primary ways that learning affects competitiveness is through its links with innovation. In today's organizations these links are typically multi-levelled (McKee 1992). They need to be understood in all their interrelatedness and complexity if they are to be fully leveraged in the generation of sustained economic performance. We see learning processes involved in innovation at the most fundamental level in an organization's research and development activity, through which it tries to generate the core scientific and technological competencies from which its future product streams will flow. We also see learning impact innovation at the business process level, as organizations seek to improve continuously the rate at which they can turn technologies into timely and successful commercial products. Finally we see learning processes impact innovation at the institutional level, where organizations set out to leverage the cumulative power of small ideas by harnessing the creative potential of all their people throughout their operations.

Innovation – competency-enhancing or competency-destroying?

We have already seen, in Chapter 2 (p. 11), how the technological trajectories of many industries follow a cyclical pattern, with long periods of continuous development punctuated by short sharp discontinuities of a frame-breaking nature. The first long period of continuous development begins after the emergence of the dominant design. It is typically characterized by incremental, competency-enhancing innovations. These industry-wide improvements occur through the interaction of many organizations. They tend to 'extend the underlying technology and thus reinforce the established technological order' (Tushman and Anderson 1986: 441). However, this situation can be radically changed by major technological advances that offer sharp price-performance improvements. The overall effect on the industry depends on whether these sharp discontinuities are competency-enhancing or competency-destroying (Abernathy and Clark 1985; Tushman and Anderson 1986). Competency-enhancing discontinuities, like the turbofan advance in jet engines, are based on know-how embodied in the technologies that they replace. Competency-destroying discontinuities on the other hand, like the electronic watch, seriously destabilize the existing industry structure by threatening to make obsolete the technological know-how of the current incumbents. The period immediately following a major technological advance is typically one of ferment in any industry, as the old technological order tries to halt the advance of the new. There is ferment also within the emerging technological order, even in the case of competency-enhancing innovation, as rival designs compete to become the new industry standard (Anderson and Tushman 1990). Learning capability, at both the technological and business process levels, is an important determinant of how any company will fare during these rare, fluid and future-defining periods.

Absorptive capacity and creative imitation

During the relatively long periods of incremental competency-enhancing innovation, the capacity to imitate creatively, using externally generated knowledge, may often be a key determinant of sustained competitiveness. Cohen and Levinthal (1990: 131) refer to an organization's ability to innovate, through the acquisition and exploitation of new knowledge, as its 'absorptive capacity'. The deeper and more diverse a firm's pre-existing knowledge structure the greater its absorptive capacity. Furthermore, absorptive capacity is a potentially difficult-to-imitate source of competitive advantage, because of its context-specific and cumulative nature, and it can be enhanced as a by-product of the firm's R&D and other knowledge-gathering activities. As Bolton (1993a) rightly points out, a strategy of learning-by-watching, as the pure importation of knowledge, confers no sustainable advantage. However, a conscious strategy of what she calls 'reflective imitation', backed up by well-developed systems and processes for exploiting externally generated knowledge, is a different matter. Reflective imitation requires the 'active adaptation of technology', the 'company-wide development of external linkages', and 'substantial investments in formal and informal strategic information systems', which cannot be purchased easily and must be developed over time. The organizational learning processes developed to turn raw imported knowledge into commercially successful products can be very proprietary. Reflective imitation processes are particularly effective in industries, like automobiles, home appliances, and electronic watches, where the basic technological order is relatively stable, incremental product development cycles are short, and speed to market is key.

At the institutional level, the growing popularity of such approaches as reverse engineering, competitive benchmarking and continuous improvement programmes is clear evidence that reflective imitation and absorptive capacity can help to leverage the cumulative power of a myriad of small ideas. In all cases the approach is only successful when the learning mind-set is institutionalized, and processes are developed to ensure that the learning can be easily transferred across the organization. As Prahalad and Hamel (1990) have pointed out, learning is in some respects analogous to money. Its impact depends not only on the stock of knowledge but also on the velocity of its circulation. At AT&T, for example, Bean and Gros (1992: 32) found that the use of 'best practice' benchmarking was at its most effective, in helping to improve the product development and other processes, only when it was 'part of a larger quality improvement programme, grounded in a quality improvement methodology common across business units'.

There are few if any businesses in which the institutionalization of a continuous improvement programme across the organization will not make an impact on a company's innovativeness and competitiveness, even in the most traditional industries. Gordon Forward, of Chaparral Steel, has recently described his company as a learning organization in which 'everybody is in research and development', and 'the plant is our laboratory' (Leonard-Barton 1992a: 29). Such an orientation is seen to be especially effective in service industries, where competency-destroying frame-breaking innovations are particularly rare. Leading retailers like Wal-Mart Stores and Marks & Spencer operate their hundreds of branches as a network of minilabs, where thousands of small, independent experiments are happening every day in diverse locations, as part of the relentless search for further improvements in merchandising and store operation. The independence and scope of the experimentation provide the requisite variety that improves the odds for success in the company-wide idea-generation process. The ability of these companies to integrate the learning from these little experiments quickly, and circulate it efficiently throughout the branch network, greatly amplifies the overall impact. The successful creation of such institution-wide learning processes is uniquely related to firm-specific systems and cultures. They are 'comprehensible only as an organic whole', and must be largely created anew by organizations that don't already have them (Leonard-Barton 1992a: 24). Since such learning processes are themselves capable of continuous improvement, as Schroeder and Robinson (1991) point out, they can offer first-mover organizations a source of competitive advantage that is not only difficult to imitate but also sustainable over the longer run.

THE LEARNING ORGANIZATION

The growing recognition of the importance of learning to innovation and competitiveness has led to a renewed interest in how individuals and organizations learn, and how these processes can be harnessed in modern organizations. While interest in how organizations, as collectives, learn is as old as organization theory itself (March and Simon 1958; Cyert and March 1963) it is only lately that it has moved to centre stage. Senge (1990a) has recently argued that the new work for strategic leadership is building the learning organization, a claim that participating organizations at the Center for Organizational Learning at MIT, like Ford, Federal Express, Philips, and Intel, would appear to wholeheartedly support.

Individual and organizational learning

While the concept of building the learning organization is a potentially attractive one for the strategy field, many important conceptual and practical challenges remain. As Kim (1993: 37) has recently pointed out, even today there remains 'little agreement on what organizational learning means and even less on how to create the learning organization'.

One central challenge is trying to understand better the link between individual and organizational learning. To begin with, we are still a long way from fully understanding the human mind, and the learning process at the individual level. Multiple theories and approaches exist, like Skinner's operant conditioning, Gestalt theory, and Freud's psychodynamics, to mention just a few. The process of how organizations learn is even less well understood. While organizations ultimately learn through individuals (Senge 1990b; Kim 1993; Dodgson 1993), it is now commonly recognized that the concept of organizational learning means more than the aggregate learning of the individual members. Organizations may not have 'brains' as such, but they do appear to have 'cognitive systems and memories', and they seem to be able to 'preserve certain behaviours' in the face of leadership changes and personnel turnover (Hedberg 1981: 3). While the notion of organizational learning is valid and useful, any such model will always have to 'resolve the dilemma of imparting intelligence and learning capabilities to a non-human entity without anthropomorphizing it' (Kim 1993: 40).

The connections between individual and organizational learning are multi-level and complex. At its most basic and obvious level, we can see organizational learning as an outcome. At this level we look primarily for the ways in which individual knowledge and behaviours are circulated, replicated and preserved in organizational contexts. We typically look to communication systems, skills training and procedural updating to help to diffuse and institutionalize such learning. This is the level at which most systematic programmes for continuous improvement concentrate, and is probably the one that is today best understood. This type of learning is typically preserved in databases and in standard operating procedures. It is at this level that modern developments in information technology will have their most immediate impact on an organization's learning capacity.

In the strategy field, as we have seen, we have become increasingly interested in organizational learning as a process, as well as an outcome. Argyris and Schon (1978) are among those who have attempted to distinguish between lower and higher levels of organizational learning, and their three-level typology, single-loop, double-loop and deutero, has since become among the most widely used. In the innovation literature, for example, McKee (1992) has associated single-loop learning with incremental product innovation and higher-level, double-loop learning with discontinuous or frame-breaking innovation. Dodgson

(1993) has equated lower-level learning with those activities that add to the knowledge base of existing firm-specific competencies, and higher-level learning with activities that fundamentally change its very nature. The lowest level of learning is mainly behavioural and adaptive. It involves adjustments to only parts of the organization, and is mainly tactical and operational in its effects. The higher levels are more cognitive and generative (Senge 1990a). They relate to fundamental readjustments throughout the organization as a whole, which are strategic in nature.

Organizational learning – challenging and changing shared 'mental models'

For organizational learning at the higher levels to occur, the firm must have a collective capacity or shared cognitive structure, capable of 'rethinking' the nature of its business, and its current strategic posture, in the most fundamental ways. Several valuable perspectives have already emerged. Shared cognitive structures have been vicariously represented as organizational ideologies (Brunsson 1982; Meyer 1982) or paradigms (Johnson 1988, 1990), particularly in the literature on change and transformation. The notion that seems to be gaining the most currency in the developing literature on organizational learning itself is the concept of the shared mental model or map (Fiol and Lyles 1985; de Geus 1988; Stata 1989; Kim 1993; Day 1994). Senge's characterization of this concept is typical: 'Mental models are deeply ingrained assumptions, generalizations, or even pictures or images that influence how we understand the world and how we take action', and 'many insights into new markets or outmoded practices fail to get put into practice because they conflict with powerful, tacit mental models' (Senge 1990b: 8).

For de Geus, Stata and others, the critical problem in strategic management today is how to accelerate the process of organizational learning. Indeed Stata has challenged the traditional thinking embodied in the experience curve, that the rate of organizational learning is primarily a function of cumulative output. 'How else', as he put it, 'can we explain the success of the Japanese automobile industry, which learned faster than the US industry with substantially less cumulative volume' (Stata 1989: 69). Modern quality improvement theory and practice shows that the rate of learning is a function of time not volume, with most improvement rates, across a wide range of businesses, fairly narrowly distributed around an average of 50 per cent every nine months (Stata 1989). Speed of higher level organizational learning is even more crucial. Organizations are having to reinvent themselves more often in today's dynamic business environment, and the ability to unearth, and change, shared mental models is seen as key to this process. As de Geus (1988: 71) has argued, the real purpose of effective strategic planning today 'is not to make plans but to change the microcosm, the mental models that [the] decision makers carry in their heads'. Successfully unearthing these shared cognitive structures, so that they can be challenged and changed, is a primary focus for those espousing a planning-as-learning philosophy. At Analog Devices, for example, two fundamental elements of the shared mental model 'melted down' under recent scrutiny, the company's 'almost fanatical commitment to decentralization', and the belief that it had to choose 'between a proprietary differentiation product strategy and a low-cost producer strategy' (Stata 1989: 67).

The process of unearthing mental models in organizations is naturally slow, because of their deep-rooted and often tacit nature. Finding new ways to accelerate this process is now seen as one of the priorities facing modern strategic management. Planners at Shell have been experimenting for some time with a more playful use of scenarios and games for this purpose (de Geus 1988). Innovative Japanese companies, like Honda and Canon, see the challenge of surfacing tacit models as 'finding ways to express the inexpressible', and approach it through using 'the store of figurative language and symbolism that managers can draw on to articulate their intuitions and insights' (Nonaka 1991: 99–100). The process through which the Honda City was created moved conceptually from metaphor through analogy to explicit model. Some deep-rooted industry-wide beliefs about the design of small cars were challenged and changed along the way. The development process was characterized by the use of such figurative language as 'let's gamble', 'theory of automobile evolution', 'man-maximum machine-minimum' and 'tall boy', at all levels of the company, and in all phases. The basic design insight that guided Canon's successful and timely reinvention from a photographic equipment to a business machine company sprung from an analogy with a beer can (Nonaka 1991).

The learning organization – a humanistic mission?

While many still see organizational learning primarily in information-processing terms (Huber 1991; Day 1994), some of the more prominent champions of the 'learning organization', or the 'knowledge-creating company', see it in more transcendent terms. For Nonaka (1991: 97), the 'knowledge-creating company is as much about ideals as it is about ideas', and 'moving from the tacit to the explicit is really a process of articulating one's view of the world', including deep-rooted values as well as conceptual insights. For Senge and his associates at MIT, the notion of the learning organization is itself an ideal to be striven for. It is based on 'a new vision of organizations, capable of thriving in a world of interdependence and change' (Kofman and Senge 1993: 5). The true learning organization, in this view, is characterized most by commitment, 'personal commitment' in the form of 'the employees' sense of identity with the enterprise and its mission' (Nonaka 1991: 97) and, even beyond this, 'commitment to changes needed in the larger world and to seeing our organizations as vehicles for bringing such changes about' (Kofman and Senge 1993: 7). Nonaka (1994: 34) sees his theory of organizational knowledge creation as, at the same time, 'a basic theory for building a truly humanistic knowledge society beyond the limitations of mere economic rationality'. For Nonaka, Senge and the others, organizations that are not able to transcend the information-processing perspective will never be able to approach the ideal of the truly learning organization, and reap the full economic as well as more spiritual benefits.

LEARNING AND COMPETITIVENESS – DEBATES AND CHALLENGES

There now seems little doubt that the learning process at individual and at institutional levels will remain a dominant theme in the competitive analysis of organizations for a long time to come, and theories of learning will become as important as theories of choice and change in the future conceptual development of the strategy process. However, there are dangers. Hawkins (1994: 71) has quite rightly cautioned that the field of organizational learning 'is still in its infancy', and in danger of suffering the fate of many management fads, where 'all too quickly' rigorous patient research is overtaken by 'evangelism and commercialization'. Others, like Ulrich *et al.* (1993: 57–8), have been concerned to ensure that emergent learning organization metaphors avoid the danger of 'concept clutter', and the trap of trying to become 'all things to all people'.

There are also tensions. Many pragmatists, like Garvin (1993: 78), are impatient with the 'reverential and utopian' discussions of the transcendents, that focus on 'high philosophy' and 'sweeping metaphors' rather than on 'the gritty details of practice'. As Ulrich *et al.* (1993: 59) have argued 'there have been far more thought papers on why learning matters than empirical research on how managers can build learning capability'. The cornerstone of the pragmatic approach is 'if you can't measure it you can't manage it' (Garvin 1993: 89). However, in Nonaka's view, the pragmatists tend to overemphasize the role of explicit knowledge and problem-solving, 'which centers on what is given to the organization – without due consideration of what is created by it' (Nonaka 1994: 14), through more tacit, experiential knowledge, rooted in the value systems of individuals. This tension has its roots in the deeper differences between traditional Western and Eastern philosophies on the processes of learning, experience and knowledge creation, and it will not be easily resolved. In spite of their differences, however, the pragmatists and trancendents do agree that the development of organizational learning capability requires a dynamic 'systems perspective', and the encouragement of greater social interaction among people from diverse functions and operations. Both requirements will be facilitated by further developments in modern information and communications technologies.

Basic philosophical tensions are not the only difficulties that beset those seeking to develop more rigorous, unified and practical theories of learning, capable of informing our understanding of the strategy process. At the heart of many models is the notion that all learning is essentially a process of experimentation and trial-and-error, with error or failure being the main source and motive for learning. At the individual level, according to Argyris (1991: 99) 'every company faces a learning dilemma: The smartest people find it hardest to learn' because they are typically the people with the least experience of failure and how to learn from it. Smart people and successful organizations are rarely forced to revisit, in any fundamental way, their basic premises and mental maps, and are often least able to do so when the need arises. Highly successful professionals and organizations are 'frequently very good at single-loop learning', but ironically this very fact helps to explain why they 'are often so bad at double-loop learning' (p. 100). This is also a dilemma at the organizational level. Must all organizations fail in order to learn, and must they fail in a very critical way before they will really fundamentally challenge and change their mental models? In the more transcendent perspectives, the use of scenarios, games and metaphors is an attempt to help successful organizations to overcome this obstacle to higher-level learning.

Finally, Hawkins (1994) and others have highlighted the danger that the current interest in learning, and its proven link with competitiveness, will lead to the view that all learning is virtuous. Leonard-Barton (1992b: 118), for example, has shown how core capabilities can often become 'core rigidities', or 'deeply embedded knowledge sets' that 'actively create problems', and need to be challenged if truly innovative product development is to occur. As Levitt and March (1988: 335) have warned, it is important to recognize that 'learning does not always lead to intelligent behaviour', and that 'the same processes that yield experiential wisdom' in organizations 'also produce superstitious learning, competency traps, and erroneous inferences'. These are just some of the potential pitfalls that the evangelists of the learning organization, in their enthusiasm for the concept, have tended to ignore.

SUMMARY

In this chapter we discussed the growing influence of the concept of learning in the strategy field. We first examined the role of learning as the source of economies of experience in traditional strategy theory. We then reviewed the increasing importance of the notion of learning in modern strategic management, first as a model of process itself (logical incrementalism/crafting metaphor), and then as a central element in modern competitive analysis, as reflected in the core competencies, activities and capabilities approaches. Some now believe that the concept of strategy as a learning process holds great promise as the basis for a more dynamic theory of strategic management. We noted that learning affects competitiveness through its links with innovation, and we examined this relationship. We saw how concepts like 'absorptive capacity' form important conceptual bridges between the two processes. We discussed the current interest in the concept of the learning organization and its potential in strategic analysis. In this regard we examined critically the relationship between individual and organizational learning, and highlighted the debate between the instrumental and visionary views of the learning organization. The chapter concluded with some further reflections on the current debates, dilemmas and conceptual challenges linking learning and competitiveness.

The relentless search for structuring arrangements that will enhance learning and innovation is one of the most important strategic challenges facing organizations in the new economic environment. In the next chapter we go on to examine this and other aspects of one of the field's most enduring themes – the relationship between strategy and structure.

Chapter 4

Structuring

In early 1988, PepsiCo undertook a major reorganization of its core beverage business in the United States, from a centralized channel focus to a decentralized regional one. It was a difficult decision, and a complex process with substantial costs and uncertain consequences. It was a significant break from the industry norm, and particularly from the type of structure that had long characterized the industry leader, Coca-Cola. PepsiCo was making a strategic investment in structural change, in the firm belief that the new organization would give it a significant competitive advantage over its great rival, for some time into the future (Pearson *et al.* 1990).

How strategic is the structuring of a company? What are the links between the patterning of a company's key intra-organizational and inter-company relationships and its competitiveness? In this chapter the relationship between strategy and structure is first examined in historical perspective, and the conceptual evolution of this relationship reviewed. The remainder of the chapter concentrates on the thematic analysis of strategies that have structures and relationships as primary elements, like vertical integration, strategic outsourcing and alliances, and diversification and decentralization.

STRATEGY AND STRUCTURE – A HISTORICAL PERSPECTIVE

The link between strategy and structure is one of the strategy field's oldest themes. Alfred Chandler's thesis that structure follows strategy was one of the seminal propositions (Chandler 1962). It quickly became embodied in the then emerging field's most dominant normative framework, the Harvard Business School model for strategy formulation and implementation (Andrews 1971). Though the direction of causality has been subsequently challenged by Burgleman (1983b), Peters (1984) and others, this relationship remains one of the dominant themes in the strategy field.

Diversification, decentralization and vertical integration

Chandler's classic study showed how desired changes in strategy, in pursuit of new opportunities arising from changes in technology and market structure, tended to press companies into new structural arrangements (Chandler 1962). Historically, new strategies of diversification seemed to require new decentralized, divisionalized forms of organization to make them effective. His strategy-follows-structure thesis was subsequently supported by French, German and British studies (Pooley-Dias 1972; Thanheiser 1972; Channon 1973). Wrigley (1970) classified large firms into single-product, dominant-product, related-product and unrelated-product categories, based on degree of diversification, and Rumelt (1974) extended this work to show how the match between diversification strategy and structure influenced economic performance. While the focus of the Wrigley–Rumelt research was on the horizontal dimension of the strategy–structure relationship, Williamson (1975) concentrated on examining the vertical dimension. He developed a transaction-cost approach to the study of vertical integration, and corporate governance, which has since become one of the most influential conceptual frameworks for subsequent research studies in this area, and the dominant paradigm in the newly emergent field of organizational economics (Barney and Ouchi 1986).

The Chandler–Wrigley–Rumelt studies of the 1970s were primarily concerned with corporate strategy, and this was almost totally equated with diversification. Their central focus was on how best to integrate diverse related and unrelated business activities within a single overall corporate structure. The dominant strategy paradigms of the time, the BCG Growth-Share Matrix and its variants (Henderson 1973; Hofer 1977; Robinson *et al.* 1978), also reflected this orientation. As Miller (1986: 233) later argued, the seminal Chandler–Wrigley–Rumelt studies 'merely scratched the surface', and there was 'clearly so much more to the concepts of both strategy and structure' than the link between product-market diversification and corporate divisionalization. For example, Waterman *et al.* (1980) argued that economic performance was dependent on the appropriate alignment of strategy with organization in a much wider sense than structure (to include systems, staff, style, skills and superordinate goals). Peters (1984: 111) further argued that 'distinctive organizational performance' was 'almost entirely a function of deeply engrained repertoires', and Burgleman (1983b) showed that many of the mechanisms developed by corporate-level management to control the implementation of current strategy also tended to shape the overall pattern of induced strategic behaviour (emergent strategy) at the divisional and business levels (see also Bower 1970). In other words, the seeds of future strategy are already deeply embedded in the current structural context, and in a very real sense not only does structure follow strategy but the reverse is also true.

Generic business strategies and configurations

In the 1980s, attention shifted to business-level strategy, as well as to wider notions of structure. These shifts opened up further perspectives on the strategy–structure relationship. Mintzberg (1981) developed a typology of structure, based on the notion of configuration, that went beyond the U-form (functionally centralized) and M-form (multi-business) categories of the Chandler–Wrigley–Rumelt era. He identified five distinct configurations, which he labelled the simple form, the machine bureaucracy, the professional bureaucracy, the divisional form and the adhocracy. Organizations, he argued, function at their most effective when they achieve internal coherence and harmony across the many organizational and administrative dimensions (reporting relationships, job specifications, spans of control, liaison devices, etc.) that constitute the wider notion of structural context discussed earlier. Around the same time, Porter (1980) developed his notion of generic strategies (low cost, differentiation and focus). These developments allowed Miller (1986) to extend our knowledge of the strategy–structure relationship to the business strategy level.

For Miller (1986: 237), 'one of the most heartening developments' to emerge from the Mintzberg and Porter work was the 'considerable overlap between the structural and strategic typologies and taxonomies'. For example, the machine bureaucracy configuration is closely matched to the requirements of a low-cost generic strategy, while the adhocracy is more consistent with innovative differentiation and the simple configuration with focus. Seen in this way, we can also say, in a very real sense, that strategy is structure and structure is strategy. Choose a low-cost strategy and you will need a machine bureaucracy configuration to make it effective; choose a machine bureaucracy as your structural configuration and, at its most effective, you will be competing on cost. The notions of structural configurations and generic strategies are complementary in other ways. Both are conceptualized as being highly stable and resistant to change. Effectiveness in both cases is based on a high degree of internal coherence and consistency. Hybrid structures and 'stuck-in-the-middle' strategies are both seen to be relatively ineffective. Migrations across types are seen to involve quite revolutionary changes, and rarely happen.

Strategy and structure – new directions and enduring issues

Our knowledge of the relationship between strategy and structure has clearly moved on considerably since the Chandler study. Indeed it has since moved on beyond the generic strategies–configurations relationships just reviewed. There are many who have taken issue with the Porter notion that companies must choose between competing on cost and competing on customization (Stata 1989; Quinn and Paquette 1990). Furthermore, Mintzberg has more recently begun to reconsider his own earlier perspective on configuration, which he now believes was too static. Organizations are continuously subject to the dynamic interplay of a number of forces, like the force for efficiency and the force for innovation, which often push in different directions. Highly stable configuration is achieved only when one force is dominant, the force for efficiency in McDonald's, say, or the force for innovation in 3M. However, there are many effective organizations where this condition is not met, and effectiveness is being achieved through the dynamic management of 'the consistency of form as well as the contradiction of forces' (Mintzberg 1991a: 66).

Most exciting of all are the new directions that research and practice are currently taking. When Chandler (1962) established his classic link between strategy and structure, he recognized that new historical developments in market structure and technology had created the opportunity for new strategies that in turn required fundamental innovations in corporate structures to make them effective. It now seems clear that a fresh historical strategy–structure cycle has been under way since the mid-1980s. Again, fundamental changes in market structure and technology are involved, though the direction of cause and effect is more difficult to determine. Are the strategies and structures of organizations being changed by these historical developments or are they driving them? The answer is probably yes to both questions, as the boundaries between organizations and their environments begin to dissolve, and the notions of the 'borderless world' and 'boundaryless corporation' enter the lexicon of modern strategic management (Ohmae 1990; Hirschhorn and Gilmore 1992).

The internationalization of competition, the globalization of scale, scope, and experience advantages, and the acceleration of microprocessor-based technological innovation are key drivers of this latest strategy–structure cycle. New leading international competitors, mainly Japanese companies, have brought with them innovations in management and organization that are rapidly diffusing throughout the industrial world. Within many organizations, the emphasis in structuring is shifting away from the vertical control of functions to the horizontal coordination of processes (Ostroff and Smith 1992). Information technology tools, like computer-aided design and computer-aided manufacturing, are facilitating greater degrees of cross-functional coordination than have ever been possible, and allowing many manufacturers to 'reengineer' their key processes, like new product development, order fulfilment, and operational logistics, for greater speed, flexibility and competitiveness (Hammer 1990). New information technologies, and the globalization of competition, are also creating 'organizational revolutions' in many service industries (Quinn and Paquette 1990). In the latest strategy–structure cycle, we are also seeing the evolution of new forms of competitive and cooperative relationships among organizations (Jorde and Teece 1989; Hamel *et al.* 1989), including the emergence of the network as a new competitive structural unit (Thorelli 1986; Jarillo 1988). Finally, our perspective on the basic unit of analysis for strategy and competitiveness is changing, from the corporate and business levels to core activities and competencies (Quinn *et al.* 1990a; Prahalad and Hamel 1990).

While the latest cycle is transforming the industrial and organizational landscapes, many of the classic themes in the strategy–structure area remain relevant. The area is still concerned with issues of diversification, decentralization and vertical integration. It is nowadays also concerned with the integration of activities across traditional functional and organizational boundaries. The remainder of the chapter will be organized around these themes, with the conceptual notions of core-competencies, transaction-cost economics and networks featuring prominently in the discussion.

VERTICAL INTEGRATION AND STRATEGIC OUTSOURCING

The strategy–structure literature has been concerned from its earliest days with vertical integration. Why do many firms tend to integrate forwards into distribution and marketing, or backwards into raw material or component manufacturing, rather than continue to rely on the external market? Until recently, a notable characteristic in economic development had been the rise of the vertically integrated corporation, and the increase in the volume of economic activity transacted within large organizations. In the 1950s, Galbraith (1956) believed that most industries were heading inexorably in the direction of greater concentration of ownership. By the late 1970s, Chandler (1977) was able to show that the 'visible hand' of management had replaced the 'invisible hand' of the market as the primary resource-allocating mechanism in the world's largest capitalist economy. However, as Peters (1992b), Carroll (1994) and others have recently demonstrated, there is much evidence to suggest that this trend has halted and, to some extent, reversed. For example, in 1954, the Fortune 500 accounted for 8 million employees and 37 per cent of America's GNP. By 1979 these figures had risen to 16 million and 58 per cent respectively. However, since then, the trend has been downwards, to 12 million employees and 40 per cent of GNP in 1991 (Peters 1992b: 9), as industries like computing were 'deconstructed', and the rules of the game changed to favour the more nimble players, with less integrated strategies (Verity 1992).

Vertical market failure

What then determines the appropriate level of vertical integration? According to Williamson (1975), the presence of vertical hierarchies in any industry represents market failure, where transaction costs for particular materials and services are higher in the marketplace than in house. Vertical markets typically fail when (i) there are only a few buyers and sellers (small numbers); (ii) supplying the product or service requires specialized investments in facilities, equipment or people skills (high asset specificity); and (iii) there are frequent transactions between the parties. These conditions tend to limit the options open to both parties and make the relationship more vulnerable to exploitation and opportunism, which increases the risks and costs of relying on the outside market. Under such conditions the transaction-cost perspective predicts that firms will be more inclined to bring the relevant transactions in house.

Vertical integration, however, can also be driven by considerations other than vertical market failure and the market power of suppliers and customers (Stukey and White 1993). A company may decide to become more integrated in order to enhance its own market power, and raise the barriers to entry for less-integrated players, as firms in the automobile industry have traditionally done through developing their own distribution and franchised dealer networks. A company may integrate backwards when its internal market for an externally sourced component or service has grown to exceed the threshold needed for minimum economic scale, as was increasingly happening, for example, with the major food and beverage customers of the US canning industry during the 1960s and 1970s (Hamermesh *et al.* 1978). Finally, a vertical integration strategy may also be driven by the stage of market development. The early producers of aluminium integrated forward into fabrication, because they believed that the downstream players had neither the incentive nor the resources to develop the market for applications at a rate that would fully exploit the potential of the then new material.

To outsource or not to outsource?

What are the drivers of the current trend towards vertical disintegration, and of the outsourcing decisions that give it effect?

Where does the balance lie?

For Chandler (1990: 132), the enduring logic of industrial success, which 'drives the creation and growth of large managerial enterprises', is the development of scale and scope in market power, and this remains 'as relevant now as it was when John D. Rockefeller put together Standard Oil'. What disintegrationists like Peters (1992b) and Quinn (Quinn *et al.* 1990a; Quinn and Hilmer 1994) take issue with is the idea that scale and scope in market power can be realized only through the existence of large managerial hierarchies. Achieving the requisite market scale without bureaucratic mass is now possible in the new industrial environment. This is a reflection of a number of developments, including the growing sophistication of many intermediate markets, the availability of new information tools, the emergence of new ways of relating within and across organizational boundaries, and the development of new perspectives on strategic outsourcing.

Sometimes new industries develop initially towards relatively high levels of vertical integration, because the scale, skills, scope and diffusion of technological know-how needed to generate viable intermediate markets take some time to develop. This was certainly true of the computer industry during the period when it was dominated by vertically integrated giants like IBM and Digital. However, the modern economic system has already developed to the stage where many intermediate markets for components and services proliferate across a wide range of activities, and many suppliers have reached levels of sophistication and scale that compare with their potential customers. At the same time, the value chains in many industries, such as computing, have now become so complex that it is increasingly difficult for any company to remain competitive across the full range of activities. These conditions are changing the basis of competition, and making outsourcing a serious strategic alternative for many companies.

For Quinn and Hilmer (1994), the new perspective on competitiveness, offered by the concepts of the value chain (Porter 1985) and activity-focused strategy (Quinn *et al.* 1990a), suggests that firms should concentrate their resources on core activities and outsource much of the rest, particularly where suitable intermediate markets exist. Sun Microsystems in computing, Nike in athletic footwear and Benetton in apparel are all examples of companies that have successfully pursued this approach. For example, Sun Microsystems had grown from start-up in the early 1980s to become a major force in the computer industry within a decade, outperforming the industry leaders in productivity and profitability, by concentrating in house on only those activities that it did best, designing microprocessors, writing software and marketing workstations. It outsourced everything from circuit-board assembly to customer support. Nike and Benetton have followed similar approaches with equally impressive results.

Such a strategy poses its own challenges. One of the most central is how to decide which activities to outsource and which to keep in house. Quinn and Hilmer (1994: 43) suggest that a company should seriously consider outsourcing any activity, except those where 'it can achieve definable preeminence and provide unique value for customers', or for which it has a 'critical strategic need'. Venkatesan (1992) advises manufacturing companies to concentrate on proprietary components that are pivotal to product differentiation (e.g. Nike sole inserts, Benetton dyes), and to outsource commodity-like components with mature technologies that add nothing to the qualities that customers consider important. Many companies over the years have systematically overinvested in new world-class manufacturing techniques and technologies, like total quality management (TQM), just-in-time (JIT) and computer-integrated manufacturing (CIM), that were misdirected at commodity parts, when the effort should have been primarily focused on 'proprietary components that could have become sources of competitive advantage' (p. 99).

Suppliers – competitors or partners?

The success of strategic outsourcing also depends on the strategic management of supplier relations. Two perspectives now dominate in the management literature, the traditional supplier-as-competitor and the more recent supplier-as-partner approaches. Porter's (1980) five-force model provides the most widely known perspective on the traditional approach. In this model a company's suppliers are seen as competitors for profit margin. Consequently, firms are advised to try to reduce the market power of their suppliers, by maintaining multiple sources of supply and by avoiding any uniqueness in the relationship in order to keep switching costs low. This is the perspective most consistent with the transaction-cost economics tradition. In it the relationship is viewed as a zero-sum game.

In the transaction-cost perspective, the risk of opportunism on the part of suppliers, defined as 'self-interest seeking with guile', is a central notion (Hill 1990: 500). This risk, according to critics, is vastly overestimated in the traditional perspective, with its narrow and negative view of human behaviour (Donaldson 1990). Institutional sociologists like Granovetter (1985) argue that the transaction-cost perspective represents an undersocialized view of human and inter-organizational interaction, that fails to take into account the embeddedness of such relationships within a wider system of social norms and values. As Jarillo (1988: 36) points out, the 'lack of trust' is seen as the 'quintessential cause of transaction costs' in the traditional view. When this assumption is relaxed, the concept of the strategic network or cluster (hub firm and supplier-partners as a competitive unit) becomes, both conceptually and practically, a viable and attractive alternative in the value-creation process to either markets or hierarchies.

The supplier-as-partner perspective is a more socialized view that sees the relationship in terms of trust, cooperation and close partnership. It is an inherent element of the Japanese just-in-time philosophy, now rapidly diffusing throughout the international economy. Its competitive potency has been demonstrated in industry after industry, from automobiles to personal computers. Indeed the Ministry for International Trade and Industry (MITI) is on record as attributing the competitive advantage of Japanese industry primarily to its subcontracting structure (Dyer and Ouchi 1993: 51). In the auto industry, for example, the Japanese manufacturers have traditionally been less vertically integrated than their American counterparts, making only 25 per cent of their component parts in house, as against nearly 50 per cent for the Detroit companies. Yet, the Japanese producers depend on a much smaller network of suppliers than the US auto-makers, and have enjoyed a 22 per cent cost advantage in their overall parts procurement and production owing to their more efficient supply system. The Japanese supplier system also supports the industry's 30 per cent faster development cycle for new products.

The emphasis in this perspective is on the development of close, cooperative, long-term relationships with a relatively small number of suppliers. It thus encourages a high degree of interdependence between company and supplier, and offers significant potential economies of cooperation to both parties. Closer coordination on schedules, cooperation on process and product innovation, and joint efforts on continuous cost reduction, all help to reduce the overall inventory investment within the company and throughout its network of suppliers. Returns to all are improved, as are quality and service to downstream customers. In short, each partner achieves many of the benefits of vertical integration with few of the risks, and the supplier becomes coopted into the buyer's competitive strategy. It all hinges on the establishment of a high degree of trust in the relationship. It requires the sharing of information and resources across organizational boundaries, which lowers the transaction costs traditionally associated with the opportunistic exploitation of information asymmetry. It also involves a willingness to co-learn and co-develop. This will inevitably lead to the generation of relationship-specific assets (knowledge, skills, physical capacity), which can only be effectively levered if trust and cooperation can be relied upon over the longer term. The 'trust dividend' can be substantial. Perhaps the greatest advantage of all, according to Quinn and Hilmer (1994: 43), will come from 'the full utilization of external suppliers' investments, innovations, and specialized professional capabilities that would be prohibitively expensive or even impossible to duplicate internally'. Furthermore, by co-developing two main suppliers for each major subsystem, as the Japanese firms typically do, companies can still ensure that some of the benefits of competition and market discipline remain in the supply system, producing 'more overall learning and innovation than would occur in a highly integrated, bureaucratic firm' (Dyer and Ouchi 1993: 58).

Critics of outsourcing point to the risk of losing key skills. Engineering and manufacturing, they argue, are not discrete functions but related bundles of skills, and it is difficult to outsource the one without damaging the other. As C.J. Van der Klugt of Philips so graphically put it, 'first you move the industrial part', then 'the development part' goes, because 'each dollar' that is paid to suppliers 'is ten cents you are giving them to develop new devices and new concepts to compete against you' (Reich and Mankin 1986: 78). Such risks can be mitigated, as Nike and Benetton have done, by keeping key proprietary components and processes in house, or by augmenting the engineering function and its links with suppliers, as Venkatesan (1992) has suggested.

There is also the danger that outsourcing will strengthen the supplier at the company's expense, as happened to IBM in its relationships with Microsoft and Intel in personal computers. Maintaining some degree of supplier-as-competitor perspective is always useful, if such risks are to be properly assessed and managed (Leavy 1994). If the transaction-cost perspective can be criticized for having an impoverished and undersocialized view of human behaviour, there is every danger that the network perspective might go too far in the opposite direction. These inter-organizational relationships will always have a political dimension, and the shifting balance of power-dependency should always remain a concern to both parties.

Horizontal integration – strategic alliances

Strategic outsourcing is not the only way that competitive value-chains are being created through partnership across organizational boundaries. Increasingly, firms are also forging such partnerships through horizontal linkages or alliances, based on shared activities. By refocusing strategic analysis on to the value-creating system itself, many companies are finding novel and competitive ways of sharing activities, and achieving an 'ever-improving fit between competencies and customers', using cooperative, interactive, strategies (Normann and Ramirez 1993: 66). Indeed, in some industries, the organizational unit of competition is no longer just the firm, but the cluster or network (Gomes-Casseres 1994). Furthermore, in some instances, as in the case of firms in Silicon Valley, production networks based on collaborative outsourcing have been instrumental in sustaining the dynamism of a whole regional economy (Saxenian 1991).

Many reasons have been advanced for the recent growth in strategic alliances. Ohmae (1989a) stresses the vast extension in new product opportunities open to companies willing to pool distinct but complementary technologies, and the significant economies of scale available to many globalizing companies willing to share many of the fixed costs involved in product development, manufacturing, marketing and distribution. In many industries, such alliances have become imperative, just to stay in the game. According to DeBresson and Amesse (1991), the presence of technological and marketing uncertainties is probably the strongest force driving companies towards cooperative strategies. For example, R&D-driven companies are increasingly collaborating in basic research activities up to the emergence of the dominant design, and then competing again once the technological trajectory becomes more predictable for all (Evan and Olk 1990). Overall, as Powell (1990: 322) points out, the conditions giving rise to cooperative strategies are 'quite diverse', but in most cases 'strategic considerations' appear to be more important than 'a simple concern with cost minimization'.

A strategic alliance can be more difficult to manage than strategic outsourcing, because it involves collaboration within, rather than across, discrete value-creating activities. In general, however, the opportunities and risks associated with each of these collaborative strategies are similar. As before, one of the primary benefits is the wider access to learning opportunities created by the alliance, and one of the main risks is the danger that the alliance might result in the emergence of a stronger and more competitive partner at the company's ultimate expense (Hamel 1991; Lei and Slocum 1992).

DIVERSIFICATION AND DECENTRALIZATION

Since its early days, the strategy–structure literature has also been preoccupied with the related themes of diversification and decentralization (Chandler 1962). In the 1960s, the decentralized, multi-divisional form of organization seemed to provide a structural innovation that could accommodate unlimited growth across a wide array of business types within a single corporate entity, and the conglomerate enterprise became a common feature on the industrial landscape. Companies like Textron developed into multi-business conglomerates that spanned such diverse activities as military helicopters, gold bracelets, chain saws, writing paper, polyurethane foam and fine china, to mention just part of the range (Bettis and Hall 1983). The arrival of the multi-business firm brought with it the need to make a distinction between corporate and business strategy. The major innovations in the strategy field of the 1970s were developed to help companies deal with the relationship between the two.

Matrix strategies and structures

The growth-share, or business portfolio, matrix was developed by

the Boston Consulting Group (BCG) to help diversifying companies to address two fundamental questions in corporate strategy:
'What businesses should the company be in?', and 'How should
corporate resources be allocated among them?' (Henderson 1973).
The BCG matrix provided a framework for managing the
corporation as a portfolio of businesses, balancing corporate cash
flow, risk and opportunity in the process. Pursuing a strategy that
balanced cash flows among the businesses ensured that management, rather than the financial markets, enjoyed the main
influence over the company's future development. The original
BCG matrix was found to be too simplistic in practice, but the
portfolio idea caught on, and a later, more sophisticated General
Electric/McKinsey version was developed, which became quite
widely used.

The portfolio approach involved organizing the multi-business
corporation into strategic business units (SBUs) for planning
purposes, based on distinct product-market focus and dedicated
resources and skills (Hall 1978). Each SBU was seen to have a
distinct strategic thrust in cash flow (net users or net generators)
and development terms (grow/hold/harvest/divest). While
there was much initial enthusiasm for the concepts of strategic
matrices and SBUs, there were many operational difficulties
which resulted in much diversity of practice. In their study of ten
firms with varying levels of experience, Bettis and Hall (1983: 97)
found that 'none of them had been successful in using the basic
model'. The main difficulties centred around trying to constitute
SBUs unambiguously as discrete businesses, limiting their
number, and dealing with the relatedness among them. Should a
company manufacturing washing machines, microwave ovens
and freezers consider each a separate SBU, or should it group them
together under appliances? Should it further distinguish between
commercial and consumer markets? Too many distinctions tended
to lead to an unmanageable number of SBUs, possibly hundreds in
the case of many large diversified companies. Too few distinctions
tended to give rise to strategies that were inappropriate because
they were too broadly applied. Treating the entire commercial
appliances business in the example above as a single cash cow SBU
might not be wise if the market prospects and competitive
strengths of the different major appliance types were quite diverse.

Many companies looked to the concept of the matrix organization to provide a structural mechanism for dealing with the

problem of relatedness among SBUs (Galbraith 1971). This idea involved the structural overlaying on a centralized functional arrangement of a decentralized business or geographical focus. Pioneers of the new arrangement, such as General Electric, Texas Instruments and Royal Dutch Shell, found that the challenges in trying to make it work were formidable. In a contemporary article, Davis and Lawrence (1978) identified a number of emergent pathologies associated with the inherent duality of the structure, including the tendencies towards anarchy, power struggles, severe groupitis, collapse during economic crunches, excessive overhead, uncontrolled layering and decision strangulation. For many companies the matrix organization has since turned out to be 'the wrong kind of complex response' to the complexities of managing a large diversified portfolio of businesses (Peters and Waterman 1982: 306), and has 'proved all but unmanageable – especially in an international context' (Bartlett and Ghoshal 1990: 139).

A resource-based perspective – portfolio of skills not businesses

Diversifying companies were primarily concerned with the question of what businesses to be in, when portfolio matrices were at the height of their popularity. The essence of corporate strategy was acquisition and divestment. However, in the early 1980s, the wisdom of extensive diversification came under new scrutiny. Nathanson and Cassano (1982), in a study of over 200 companies, found that returns had actually declined with increasing product diversity, while remaining relatively steady as market diversity increased. Porter (1987: 43) likewise discovered that the 'track record' of corporate strategies was 'dismal', even in many of the most prestigious companies. The average rate of subsequent divestment for acquisitions into unrelated businesses was almost three quarters. In short, 'extremely profitable base businesses' had 'subsidized poor diversification track records', in many leading companies like CBS and General Mills (p. 45).

For Porter, many companies looked to diversification for future growth, without any in-depth evaluation of how the existing corporate entity actually hoped to add value to the acquired businesses. He posed three essential tests for successful diversification: (i) the attractiveness test – the structural attractiveness (in five-force terms) of the industry into which the company is planning to diversify; (ii) the cost of entry test – to ensure that the company does not capitalize all the future profits by paying too high an entry price; and (iii) the better-off test – in terms of how the newly acquired business can gain competitive advantage from links with the corporation and/or vice-versa (economies of scale and scope, and/or the transfer of learning). Meeting these three tests, 'which set the standards' for any corporate strategy, 'is so difficult that most diversification fails' (p. 49). Furthermore, the traditional portfolio approach to corporate strategy and diversification does little to address them.

Diversification strategies have also failed because of the difficulties inherent in actually managing diversity. What Campbell *et al.* (1995) have recently referred to as the 'parenting advantage' is not easily realized across different business types. For example, the British conglomerate BTR was surprised to find that its successful corporate 'formula' for diversified manufacturing did not readily extend to distribution. ICI's recent decision to demerge into two separate parent companies, 'new' ICI and Zeneca, reflected similar difficulties with the management of diversity (Owen and Harrison 1995). According to Prahalad and Bettis (1986), much of the explanation linking diversification and performance may reside in the shared organizational schemata, cognitive maps or 'dominant logics' of the corporate management team. Strategic rather than product/market variety may be the limiting factor that determines how much diversity any given corporate team can manage successfully. A high degree of product relatedness among businesses is one way to reduce the strategic variety to manageable proportions. However, an equally effective way might be to try to achieve a similar strategic emphasis (low-cost or differentiation) across the diverse businesses, as companies like Emerson Electric have traditionally tried to do. 'The bottom line', Prahalad and Bettis believe, 'is that each management team at a given point in time has an inbuilt limit to the extent of diversity it can manage' (p. 497). Relatedness 'may be as much a cognitive concept as it is an economic or technical one', and the capacity to add or change dominant logics, in order to extend the amount of strategic variety that can be managed, may 'revolve around the ability of the firm or its dominant coalition to learn' (pp. 497–9).

According to Prahalad and Hamel (1990), some of the most

successful diversified companies control strategic variety by reconceiving the corporation in terms of a portfolio of core skills and competencies rather than businesses. In their perspective, corporate strategy takes on a deeper meaning and a more direct link with overall competitive advantage. The central question is no longer 'What businesses are we going to be in?', but 'Upon what deeply-layered, enduring and enhanceable core competencies are we going to build the future of the corporation?' While few companies are likely to build world leadership in more than five or six fundamental competencies, this limited set, if strategically chosen, should provide potential access to a wide variety of markets. In this view, competitiveness derives from 'management's ability to consolidate corporatewide technologies and production skills' into core competencies that can 'spawn unanticipated products' (p. 81). For Stalk *et al.* (1992) the route to successful diversification is seen to be similar. A strategic focus on transferable core capabilities will allow a company to compete 'in a remarkable diversity of regions, products, and businesses and do it far more coherently than the typical conglomerate can' (p. 65).

For these theorists the concepts of business portfolio and SBUs may be harmful to their more integrative view of corporate strategy. In the core competencies/capabilities view, business strategies grow out of corporate strategy, and not the other way round. In corporations managed primarily through the SBU concept, top management tends to focus only on the product-market level of competitiveness at the expense of the other two levels, core products (such as Honda engines and powertrains) and core competencies or capabilities (such as Honda technologies or Wal-Mart logistics). The 'fragmentation' of such core competencies becomes 'almost inevitable' where the information systems, patterns of communication, career paths, and processes of strategy development 'do not transcend SBU lines' (Prahalad and Hamel 1990: 89). As a result, resources tend to become imprisoned within SBUs, core competencies underdeveloped, and innovation too narrowly defined. However, the core competencies approach is not without its critics. According to Campbell *et al.* (1995: 120), the approach 'has not provided practical guidelines' for developing corporate-level strategy, 'despite its powerful appeal', nor does it fully address the corporate-level strategic issues that face companies like ABB and General Electric, whose businesses have 'limited technical or operating overlap'. Such companies are also seeking the solution to the strategic management of diversity in new approaches to organizational structure and processes, as we shall see a little later on.

The headquarters–subsidiary/business unit relationship

One of the most enduring structural issues in the management of diversity is the headquarters–subsidiary/business unit relationship. Finding the right balance between centralization and decentralization remains the major challenge. While Siemens decentralizes, Matsushita reconsolidates. Companies still 'swing like a pendulum and never seem to get it right' (Ghoshal and Mintzberg 1994: 8). This should not surprise us because, as Percy Barnevik of ABB recently pointed out, the modern diversified multinational company typically faces three internal contradictions, how to be 'big and small', 'global and local' and 'radically decentralized with centralized reporting and control' (Taylor 1991: 95). At Xerox, CEO Paul Allaire has been trying to find 'the best of both worlds – the speed, flexibility, accountability, and creativity that come from being part of a small, highly-focused organization, and the economies of scale, the access to resources, and the strategic vision that a large organization can provide' (Howard 1992: 111).

The appropriate relationship between corporate headquarters (HQ) and the business units or subsidiaries seems to depend on the type of corporation and the nature of its development. Goold and Campbell (1987) identified three distinct styles of relationship typical of British firms: Strategic Planning, Strategic Control and Financial Control. Chandler (1991: 36) compared the British and US experiences, and concluded that these different styles tended to 'result from different paths to growth, and therefore, from different patterns of investment and from different sets of organizational capabilities'. In Financial Control companies, corporate control was exercised mainly through the annual budget, with responsibility for business strategy almost totally devolved to units. This arm's-length approach is only effective in service industries, or in industries with relatively inexpensive production facilities and small R&D expenditures, and is often found in true conglomerates, like Hanson Trust. The Strategic Planning and Strategic Control styles, typified by the approaches of BP and ICI respectively, involve greater degrees of involvement by HQ in the development and coordination of business unit strategies. However, even here, Gould (1991: 76) found that informal strategic controls seemed to predominate, especially in companies where there were 'strong linkages between businesses in the corporate portfolio, high levels of uncertainty, and multiple, complex, hard-to-measure sources of competitive advantage'.

The appropriate level of control between HQ and the businesses may vary over time, and across the company, with a unit's stage of development. This seems particularly apt in the case of many globalizing service industries, like fast-food, where diversification into new markets is based on the expansion of a branch network of highly replicable operations. The initial priority on entering a new region is to test the basic service concept in the new territory. Later, if the concept is found to be viable, the priority shifts to expanding the branch network in order to stake out the territory and get good market coverage before serious competition takes hold. Finally, when the rate of expansion in the number of outlets begins to slow, the commercial priority shifts to operating performance for cash and profit generation. In the first stage the emphasis at HQ should be primarily on financial control, giving the local unit seed capital and allowing it the strategic and operational latitude to experiment and learn about the local market. In the expansion stage the funding requirements of the subsidiary should be assessed in terms of overall corporate and business priorities and imperatives, and some degree of strategic control seems appropriate – should the subsidiary manage its own growth or should HQ continue to support it with additional capital and skills? It is at the third stage that subsidiary performance can be most greatly leveraged by tighter strategic and operational integration with the rest of the network, exploiting to the full the kind of economies of scale, scope and experience typically available to such service companies (Quinn and Paquette 1990).

A federal alternative?

Diversified corporations continue to search relentlessly for the best balance between centralization and decentralization. In addition, most internationalizing companies want to be both globally efficient and locally flexible. Reconciling all of these tensions through structure alone is difficult. Many companies see some form of matrix organization as the only option, whatever the shortcomings. However, Doz and Prahalad (1991: 146) point out that advocating the matrix form is just an acknowledgement of the 'structural indeterminacy' inherent in these tensions, and they emphasize the need to focus more 'on underlying processes' in the search for their resolution.

There is now growing evidence that diversified multinational corporations like ABB, General Electric, IBM and Xerox are moving beyond the traditional matrix form, in terms of key processes and systems as well as structure (Bartlett and Ghoshal 1993). At the heart of these changes is a transformation in the role of corporate leader, and in the relationship between the corporate centre and the businesses. Corporate management, according to Chandler (1991), has always been about two functions, value creation (entrepreneurial) and loss prevention (administrative). What these modern corporations are now trying to do is to devolve both of these functions and make them more effective. At General Electric, for example, Jack Welch has been trying to 'create an enterprise that can tap the benefits of global scale and diversity without the stifling costs of bureaucratic controls and hierarchical authority' (Tichy and Charan 1989: 112). All of them are moving towards federalist solutions. To Handy (1992) this represents a significant conceptual and practical departure in organizational life. It is a philosophical, and not just a structural, solution. The basic principles of federalism, that autonomy releases energy; that people have the right to do things in their own way as long as it is in the common interest; that people need to be well informed, well intentioned and well educated to interpret that common interest; that individuals prefer being led to being managed, all seem to be in tune with the needs, demands and paradoxes of modern corporate life.

The ABB 'federation' consists of nearly 1,200 companies with on average 200 employees. These are as far as possible separate legal entities with real balance sheets, and real responsibility for cash flow and dividends. These companies are geographically coordinated by country managers, and globally coordinated by business area leaders. Headquarters for the entire corporation consists of just 100 people. The fifty business area leaders are responsible for strategy and global optimization at business level, and the thirteen members of the executive committee, each responsible for a business segment, a region and some administrative functions, are collectively responsible for the corporation's global strategy and performance (Taylor 1991). In a similar way, the entrepreneurial function has been almost totally devolved to the businesses in General Electric and Xerox. The main responsibility of HQ is to try to create the systems and processes that will help the business managers and corporate staff specialists to develop an overall sense of collective responsibility for the future of the corporation. At General Electric the federal perspective is developed and nurtured through the Corporate Executive Council, the collective forum of business leaders and corporate staff which 'creates a sense of trust, a sense of personal familiarity and mutual obligation at the top of the organization', and helps to ensure 'the transfer of best practices across all the businesses, with lightning speed' (Tichy and Charan 1989: 115–16). A further dimension of the federal approach is evident at Xerox, where the corporate management no longer sets resource allocation priorities in traditional top-down fashion, but encourages the business leaders to approach them as entrepreneurs might approach venture capitalists (Howard 1992).

The new federalist approach does not eliminate the tensions inherent in the matrix organization. Rather it internalizes them in the roles of key managers. At ABB, the presidents of the local companies are expected to handle the ambiguity associated with having dual reporting relationships. Likewise at Xerox the company expects its division people to be able to manage the tension between autonomy and integration that is built into their new roles. The challenge, as one senior executive expressed it, is 'not so much to build a matrix structure as it is to create a matrix in the minds of our managers' (Bartlett and Ghoshal 1990: 145). The successful implementation of federalism involves holistic attention to structure, management skills and culture, and cannot be successful without a mutually supporting transformation in all three areas. It is not so much a structure as 'a way of life', which reaches into the 'soul' of the organization (Handy 1992: 60). It is a perspective that 'reverses a lot of traditional managing thinking', and now seems to be infusing fresh life into the strategy–structure debate (p. 72).

SUMMARY

In this chapter we examined the strategic significance of organizational structuring and the links between the patterning of intra-firm and inter-firm relationships and company competitiveness. The evolution of the strategy–structure theme was reviewed in historical perspective. Traditionally it was found to be almost totally concerned with the link between decentralization and diversification in corporate strategy, and to a lesser extent with vertical integration. More recently the theme has expanded to include the relationship between generic business strategies and internal business unit configurations, linking Porter's ideas on strategy with Mintzberg's on structure. We noted the trend towards vertical disintegration in the new economy, and critically examined the strategic potency of the new partnership arrangements, both vertical (strategic outsourcing) and horizontal (strategic alliances), highlighting the major opportunities and risks involved. Finally we examined the relationship between decentralization and diversification, highlighting the traditional difficulties with matrix strategies and structures, assessing the more recent concern about the capacity of the firms to manage diversity successfully, analysing the changing nature of the headquarters–subsidiary relationship over time and the appropriate levels of control, and noting the most recent trend towards federalism.

The importation of federalism into organizational life, if fully embraced, would be a new departure. It heralds the arrival of a less instrumental and more value-driven view of structuring and its relationship with organizational strategy and purpose. Value-driven views will feature even more prominently in the next chapter, as we now move on to examine the importance of leadership and culture to strategy and competitiveness.

Chapter 5

Leadership and culture

Few areas in the purview of business and society have been more engaging than leadership. In generation after generation, the yearning for leadership seems to be persistent, yet rarely satisfied. In the late 1940s, for example, contemporary experts believed that there was 'an unconscious search for leaders' in that 'age of social ferment' (Gras 1949: 419). Four decades later, they were just as convinced that 'if there was ever a moment in history when a comprehensive strategic view of leadership was needed' then the mid-1980s was 'certainly it' (Bennis and Nanus 1985: 2). The phenomenon of leadership seems central, yet it has proved itself to be quite intractable to research. Many significant questions remain unanswered. What are the distinguishing characteristics of leadership, and why has it been so difficult to isolate them? Is good leadership easily transferable across different businesses or even different strategies? Are leaders and managers different? Is leadership more symbolic than substantial? How is leadership linked to culture, and how are both linked to sustained economic performance? These issues will be the main focus of this chapter.

WHAT IS LEADERSHIP?

Over 5,000 studies to date, and many decades of research, have failed to provide definitive answers to basic questions such as 'What distinguishes effective from ineffective leaders?'. As Meindl *et al.* (1985: 78) so aptly put it, 'after years of trying, we have been unable to generate an understanding of leadership that is both intellectually compelling and emotionally satisfying', and the concept remains 'largely elusive and enigmatic'. Stogdill (1974: 259), in one of the most comprehensive reviews of the leadership literature, noted that 'there are almost as many definitions of leadership as there are persons who have attempted to define the concept'. In short, the phenomenon is complex, and there are many ways of looking at it. Most have provided some insight, none has been comprehensive (see Jago 1982 and Yukl 1989 for two more recent reviews).

The early attempts to understand leadership concentrated on personal characteristics such as traits and behaviours. The early trait studies, which often took the great leaders of history such as Washington, Gandhi and Churchill as their subjects, tended to concentrate on areas of general intelligence and personality. They were largely inconclusive. The implicit theory in many of these approaches was that great leaders are born, not made. With the advent of managerialism, the emphasis shifted from attributes to behaviours. The needs of the modern corporation required that research should concentrate on how to improve the basic leadership competencies of the many, rather than merely trying to understand the distinguishing attributes of the outstanding few. Research on leadership became almost totally centred on middle management. It became preoccupied with trying to establish which of two main styles, directive or participative, was the most effective. The subsequent recognition that neither style was universally superior led to the development of the situational-contingency theories of Fiedler (1967), and others.

Is the effective leader a readily transferable asset?

One of the earliest beliefs in modern management was that the accomplished leader could be equally effective across a wide range of organizations and industries. It was a belief that helped to fuel the conglomerate growth of the 1960s and 1970s. Fiedler's was one of the earliest perspectives to question this view. Furthermore, he argued that companies should learn how to 'engineer the job to fit the manager', since it was 'surely easier to change almost anything in the job situation than a man's personality and his leadership style' (Fiedler 1965: 115). Other influential contemporaries believed that individuals were much more flexible in their ability to vary their style to suit the situation (Tannenbaum and Schmidt 1958).

There has since been much evidence to suggest that individual leaders are unlikely to be equally effective across industries, companies or even strategies. Shetty and Perry (1976), for example, in an extensive study of nearly 300 chief executives, found that only around 10 per cent of them had transferred in directly from different companies and about 5 per cent from unrelated industries. For these researchers, leadership effectiveness was rooted in the development over time of firm- and industry-specific knowledge and relationships, as well as in generic competencies. Kotter's later study tended to confirm and extend this view (Kotter 1982). His was one of a number of subsequent studies that began to place more emphasis on leadership as an activity or process, with a concern for what leaders actually do and how they do it, as well as for their personal attributes and styles. For Kotter, the general management process was one of developing a strategic agenda over time (which may not be fully reflected in the formal planning process for sound political reasons) and the patient development of the network of supporting relationships needed to carry it through. In this perspective, the leader's business-specific knowledge and connections are clearly seen as leverageable assets that are not always readily transferable across different contexts and situations.

An emerging process view

The early attempts to examine leadership as a process remained very person-centred in orientation, and continued to seek the explanation for effectiveness primarily within the behaviour repertoires and skills of the individual. Later research has since tried to widen the perspective by examining the dynamics of leadership within the larger process of strategy formation (Leavy and Wilson 1994). When viewed in this way, the legacy of any leader is seen to be a product of three elements, the person, the organization and the historical challenge facing both. Some leaders, for example, will be remembered in the future history of their organizations as builders or revitalizers, not only because of their personal capacities for such roles, but also because of the opportunities presented to them by history and context. There is an organizational equivalent to the observation by Richard Nixon (1982: 2), in the public policy field, that 'placing a leader among the greats has three elements: a great man, a great country and a great issue'. This is not just a 'horses for courses' view in the traditional situational-contingency sense, but a more dynamic and richly contextual 'heroes for historical moments of truth' perspective (Leavy 1995). Some leaders may not be given the opportunity by history to distinguish themselves fully; others may simply not be up to the challenges presented to them.

This view sees leadership effectiveness located in the interaction of leader, organization and context over time. The focus of interest shifts beyond attributes and skills to the dynamics of performance. It is akin to the institutionalist view of leadership of Biggart and Hamilton (1987), and the views of leadership as drama and performing art of Vaill (1989), Westley and Mintzberg (1989), and Starrat (1993). It recognizes that the leadership role, as most incumbents find it, can already be quite heavily scripted by 'the historical legacy of role expectations and interactional heritage of a specific organization or society' and the 'social and cultural beliefs and values' within which it is 'embedded' (Biggart and Hamilton 1987: 435–7). For example, the presidencies of George Washington and Ronald Reagan in the United States were very different, not least because of the differences in role expectations attaching to the position in different historical contexts. Yet history and context never totally define the leadership process. As Biggart and Hamilton (1987: 437) put it, leadership, however constrained, 'always involves creative performances', and to miss this personal performance element is to 'miss the entire phenomenon, for leadership is only manifest in interaction'. Mary Robinson's imaginative leadership within the very institutionally constrained office of the Irish Presidency is a good illustration.

The process/performance view brings into focus the issue of whether leadership effectiveness varies over tenure. Some time ago, Eitzen and Yetman (1972) found a curvilinear pattern between coaching tenure and team performance in US college basketball, with performance rising to a peak over the first thirteen years or so, and then going into steady decline. Hambrick and Fukutomi (1991) have recently found a similar pattern in the tenures of many long-serving chief executives. These executives, it seems, first grow in the job, and their effectiveness increases with this learning process. Then they tend to grow 'stale in the saddle' (Miller 1991), and become victims of their own earlier success. Success 'increases the credibility and independence of leaders and makes them overconfident and complacent' (p. 35). As their power and reputations grow, their views become less likely to be challenged from within or without. They and their organizations become less responsive, and the likelihood of a serious mismatch developing between the organization and its environment increases.

In sum, the emergent process/performance view is raising promising fresh angles on a much-studied phenomenon that remains as intriguing as it has been intractable.

LEADERS AND MANAGERS – ARE THEY DIFFERENT?

Are managers and leaders different? Since the late 1970s, this has been one of the most enduring questions in the field (Zaleznik 1977, 1992). Before that, leadership research was primarily concerned with middle management and small group dynamics, and strategy research was more concerned with techniques than with leadership. As Hambrick (1989: 5) recently noted, top management 'became noticeably absent from writings on strategy, somehow passed over in favour of more techno-economic factors such as product life cycles, market share, experience curves, portfolio matrices, and industry analysis'. In the mid-1980s, the emergence of high-involvement, high-performance organiza- tions, like Wal-Mart, Microsoft and The Body Shop, changed all that. Sam Walton, Bill Gates, Anita Roddick and others like them forced the strategy field to take a renewed interest in the relationship between leadership and sustained economic success. According to Zaleznik (1992), the notion that managers and leaders were different was largely rejected in the prevailing 'managerial mystique' of the late 1970s, when his classic article first appeared. It is being taken much more seriously today.

Recently there has been a growing recognition that top leadership might be different in kind as well as degree from the rest of management, and top leaders a 'breed apart' (Norburn 1989). Bennis and Nanus (1985: 21) have argued that there is a 'profound difference between management and leadership', and that most underperforming organizations are typically 'over- managed and underled'. Leaders focus on effectiveness ('doing the right things'), and managers on efficiency ('doing things right'), two fundamentally different orientations. According to Kotter (1990: 103–4) they are 'distinct systems of action', with management being about 'coping with complexity' while leader- ship is about 'coping with change'. However, he tends to reject strongly the notion that the same individual cannot be effective in both roles.

According to Zaleznik (1977, 1992), leaders and managers are different in fundamental personality type and psychological perspective. Managers are typically 'once-born' personalities who fully belong in their social surroundings, and are good social and political operators in a relatively detached sort of way. Leaders, in contrast, tend to be 'twice-born' personalities characterized by a profound sense of separateness, who 'may work in organizations, but never belong to them', and their lives are often typified by internal struggle, neurosis or magnificent obsession (Zaleznik 1992: 132; Noel 1989). Certainly there are many leaders, like Ted Turner and Steve Jobs, who seem to fit the 'twice-born' profile, and it is interesting to note that many leaders have pointed to some disruption during their formative years as defining episodes in their careers (Sims 1993). However, Zaleznik offered Alfred Sloan as his supreme example of the 'once-born' managerial type. That Sloan, who is generally recognized as one of the great strategists in the history of the automobile industry, can be said to have been a manager but not a leader is the kind of assertion that gives a real edge to this debate.

One of the most interesting perspectives on this debate was provided by James McGregor Burns (1978) in the public policy literature. Burns drew an insightful distinction between two types of leadership, transactional and transformative, which has since proved very influential in the strategy field (Bennis and Nanus 1985; Roberts 1985; Tichy and Devanna 1986; Kuhnert and Lewis 1987; Leavy 1992). Transactional leadership is the most common type found in organizational life. It is rooted in a direct exchange relationship between leader and follower, and is relatively independent of history and context. Transactional leadership motivates by means of concrete economic (salary/promotion) or psychological (mutual loyalty/respect) exchanges, which are an accepted part of the management process at all levels. Transformative leadership, on the other hand, operates out of deeply held personal value systems that cannot be negotiated or exchanged. Where transactional leadership induces, transformative leadership inspires. Transformative leadership reaches out beyond the immediacy of face-to-face interaction to infuse entire organizations with a collective sense of mission and purpose. There are clear parallels with the Zaleznik perspective. As Kuhnert and Lewis (1987: 649) characterize them, 'transactional and transformative leaders are qualitatively different kinds of individuals who construct reality in markedly different ways'.

IS LEADERSHIP KEY TO SUPERIOR ECONOMIC PERFORMANCE?

Even if leadership is different, how important is it as a source of sustainable competitive advantage? How distinctive an asset is the leadership of Bill Gates to Microsoft, or Richard Branson to Virgin?

In the early 1970s, Lieberson and O'Connor (1972) found that chief executive succession appeared to have very little effect on overall firm performance, relative to environmental factors. In the days of the 'managerial mystique', when the organization as efficient machine was the dominant metaphor, this was probably a comforting finding. To those of a scientific management orientation, individual talent had always been seen as an unpredictable and unreliable basis on which to secure the future of a corporation. However, the study has since been replicated in various different ways and contexts, with somewhat conflicting results, which add fuel to the debate. Thomas (1988: 338) even reinterpreted the original findings, and argued that they actually provided 'compelling evidence that individual leaders do make a difference'. The link between chief executive succession and firm performance has continued to be a major focus for study (Dalton and Kesner 1985; Zajac 1990; Wiersema 1992). While the debate remains unresolved, what does seem clear is that the relatively high level of CEO turnover in Western business reflects, at the very least, a widely shared belief that individual leadership does make a difference.

Symbol and substance – charismatic leadership

In the late 1970s, Pfeffer and Salancik's resource-dependence theory argued that organizations are much less self-directed than many of their constituencies would care to believe or accept (Pfeffer and Salancik 1978). It also argued that leadership was more about perception than substance. Others have since supported this view. For example, Czarniawska-Joerges and Wolf (1991: 529) believe that leadership is largely 'symbolic performance, expressing the hope of control over destiny'. It often assumes a 'romanticized, larger-than-life role' in 'after the fact' accounts of organizational outcomes (Meindl *et al.* 1985: 79). However, the emergence of high-commitment, high-performance organizations like Wal-Mart and The Body Shop, during the 1980s, brought with it a rising interest in the social anthropology or culture of organizations, including the norms, values, heroes, myths and beliefs that bind them together as communities of action (Peters and Waterman 1982; Deal and Kennedy 1982). This helped to divert the focus of the symbol-or-substance debate on to the more interesting and complex issue of how the symbolic and substantive elements of leadership interact to produce outcomes of strategic significance (Leavy 1995a).

The growing interest in the symbolic, and its role in organiza-tions like Wal-Mart and Microsoft, also brought with it a renewed interest in the phenomenon of charismatic leadership (Conger and Kanungo 1987; House *et al.* 1991; Bryman 1993). According to Bryman (1993), charismatic leaders have at least three notable characteristics: they are regarded as exceptional, they have a vision or mission that elicits followership, and they enjoy great personal loyalty and high levels of commitment from their followers. The willingness to pursue the shared vision in a disinterested manner, and at great personal risk and sacrifice, is often seen as one of the key sources of their charisma. They are seen more as 'active innovators', rather than as 'group facilitators, like consensual leaders' (Conger and Kanungo 1987: 643). Bill Gates seems typical of the genre. According to one of his senior lieutenants, Gates is 'incredibly important' (Appleyard 1994: 22). He is 'one of the smartest people of the 20th century' with a 'historical level of genius', and his loyal followers compete for his respect (p. 22). If anything happened to Gates 'the company would go on all right, but after a while we'd be afraid to make the big bets' (p. 25). Such leaders are seen to 'affect followers in ways that are quantitatively greater and qualitatively different than the effects specified by past leadership theories' (House *et al.* 1991: 364). And even if the qualities attributed to the charismatic leader are somewhat mythical, it may well be that 'the romance and the mystery' are 'critical for sustaining followership and that they contribute significantly to the responsiveness of individuals to the needs and goals of the collective organization' (Meindl *et al.* 1985: 100).

Vision, values, conviction and strategic intent

Whether charisma of the more mythical type is the distinguishing feature of exceptional leadership is still open to debate (Kotter 1990). However, many now believe that such leaders (charismatic or not) are most marked by their ability to endow their organizations with a strong sense of vision and mission (Bennis and Nanus 1985; Tichy and Devanna 1986; Nanus 1992). Indeed, it could be argued that in today's organizations 'the concepts of leadership and strategy have been combined into that of strategic vision', where leadership is seen to engender strategic thinking and initiative at many levels of the organization rather than formulating strategy in the more traditional, highly directive way (Westley and Mintzberg 1989: 17). According to Jack Welch of General Electric: 'Good business leaders create a vision, articulate the vision, passionately own the vision, and relentlessly drive it to completion' (Tichy and Charan 1989: 113). Westley and Mintzberg (1989: 19) now see vision as expressing the essential artistry of strategic leadership, 'not the vision as a private mental image' so much as the vision 'articulated' and 'communicated in words and actions'.

Where does the capacity for visionary leadership come from, and how is it developed? Many have turned to a variety of mind-expanding techniques, such as lateral thinking, in the elusive search for the 'vision thing'. Nanus (1992: 182) has even attempted to offer ambitious parents some guidance on how to develop in their 'youngsters' the intellectual and social skills that will prepare them for future 'roles as visionary leaders'. However, the concentration on generic skills, implied in these responses, can only take us so far. According to Collins and Porras (1991: 31) most corporate vision statements 'are terribly ineffective as a compelling guiding force', and have little real 'gut-grabbing' meaning. There is now a growing recognition that inspirational leadership is rooted in values, convictions and principles of a more spiritual and aesthetic nature. 'Vision that is not centred in a profound spirituality is nothing more than a pictorial might-be', according to Vaill (1989: 223). People in the workplace are increasingly looking to the organization's leaders for a sense of institutional purpose that helps 'give meaning to people's lives' (Bartlett and Ghoshal 1994: 86). They want a covenant with their leaders, and not just a contract (de Pree 1989). As the late Jean Riboud of

Schlumberger once observed, the reason why many Japanese companies emerged as world-class competitors in the last two decades is that 'they had the same faith that the great religions had in past centuries' (Auletta 1991: 418). In a similar vein, what Hamel and Prahalad (1989) have called strategic intent, or great ambition, may also be more easily recognized than replicated. It may be that the recent success of companies like Honda, Canon and Komatsu can only be fully understood when seen in the overall context of Japan's historic 'targets' for 'overtaking the West' and restoring national pride (Horsley and Buckley 1990: 141).

The great ambitions and compelling visions of truly inspirational leadership appear to have their roots in history and context, and help to give a deeper meaning to contemporary experience (Leavy 1992; Leavy and Wilson 1994). This is why the attempt to teach vision as a generic management skill seems doomed to have at best only limited success. Leaders of vision do not merely see possibilities that the rest of us, with much narrower horizons, have never dreamed of, but are also moved by deeply held convictions to make them happen. Leaders, whose interests remain too narrow, and whose own deeper values remain unknown and untouched, are unlikely to be able to provide the kind of compelling vision that will really make a difference. To a large extent, truly inspirational leadership may remain a gift of history. In so far as it can be consciously developed, then the type of liberal education that helps individuals to explore their own deeply held values and beliefs, and connect with their own culture and the sweep of human history, would seem to offer the most fruitful route. Only through such a process can leaders come to appreciate more fully 'that their power does not come from the force of their personalities, but from the power of values that ground human life as meaningful and worthwhile' (Starrat 1993: 137).

LEADERSHIP AND CORPORATE CULTURE

Since the early 1980s, many, like Deal and Kennedy (1982: 5), have come to view 'strong culture' as the 'driving force behind continuing success'. The concepts of transformational leadership and corporate culture are inextricably linked, and the revival of interest in the role of charisma and vision in leadership studies is a reflection of the belief that 'much if not most of what matters in organizational life takes place at the cultural level' (Louis 1981:

250). Both concepts brought people, as individuals and collectives, back to centre stage in what Ebers (1985) characterized as the new 'Romanticism' in modern organizational analysis. Both characterized a distinct break with traditional instrumental views of leadership, strategy and organization in favour of a perspective concerned with how vision, meaning and symbolic action help to 'integrate individuals, organization and environment into an organic whole' (Ebers 1985: 55). As Starrat (1993: 5) put it 'leadership in the cultural perspective is exercised not so much by scientific management as by guarding essential values of the culture'. In a very real way, such leadership involves the embodiment of organizational values and purpose (Selznick 1957).

Institutionalizing the founding charisma – corporate culture

How do organizations survive beyond the tenures of the charismatic founders, whose visionary leadership is linked with their outstanding success? How much of Wal-Mart's uniqueness will survive and for how long, now that Sam is dead? Even during a founder's tenure these 'vibrant, almost cult-like', organizations are often seen to lose some of their 'sparkle' owing to the pressures for formalization that come with growth (Bryman 1993: 294). When such pressures lead to the founder's departure, the effect can be traumatic, leaving devotees disoriented and confused. When Steve Jobs left Apple, some believed that they had 'cut the heart out of Apple', and wondered how long the 'artificial' substitute would continue to pump (Uttal 1985: 12).

Whatever the difficulties, organizations that have successfully institutionalized their visionary capability and compelling sense of mission are evident across a wide range of industry and national contexts, as Collins and Porras (1991) have shown. They are typically characterized by enduring guiding philosophies derived from their entrepreneurial founders. Sometimes these philosophies are written down, but more often than not, like the 'H-P Way' of Hewlett-Packard, they just seem 'built in and understood', as Bill Hewlett himself recently described it (Collins and Porras 1991: 36). Likewise the 'spirit of Hondaism' is seen to be open to 'many interpretations', and can never simply be reduced to 'a fixed set of rules' (Mito 1990: 1). At Herman Miller, 'a very diverse group of individuals' shares a 'set of common values', the roots of which

may 'differ from person to person', but the 'spoken and understood expressions of it are remarkably coherent' (de Pree 1989: 82).

Within such companies, the leadership process itself is often
seen in primarily cultural terms. 'The first responsibility of a
leader', according to Max de Pree (1989: 11), 'is to define reality.'
The strong sense of internal cultural cohesiveness is often related
to a distinctive history, and to the founding vitality preserved in its
transmission. At companies like Marks & Spencer, Lincoln
Electric, Honda and The Body Shop, the founding philosophies
often ran counter to the norms of the time. Cultural distinctiveness
was often the most enduring source of their differentiation
advantages. The Marks & Spencer commitment to partnership
with employees and suppliers was well ahead of its time in
Western business, as was the Lincoln Electric commitment to
customers and employees as the primary stakeholders in the
business. Honda's founding commitment to originality and
individualism ran counter to the norms in Japanese industry,
while Anita Roddick just tended to 'look at what the cosmetic
trade [was] doing and walk in the opposite direction' (Campbell
1994: 664). Successors in such companies tend to see their own
missions in terms of preserving and transmitting the founding
culture. At Honda, for example, Kiyoshi Kawashima was
'fanatical' about putting the company's founding mottoes and
principles into action (Mito 1990: 7). According to de Pree (1989:
82), the penalty facing any company that fails to preserve the
'tribal' lore is to 'lose one's history, one's historical context, one's
binding values'.

Companies led through a cultural perspective typically pay a
lot of attention to the selection and socialization of their employees
(Pascale 1985). Somewhat like religious or political movements,
they tend to attract and hire kindred spirits. For example, Honda
developed its somewhat distinctive culture because its founder
deliberately hired other mavericks who were typically college
dropouts or rejects from traditional, more established companies
(Pearson and Ehrlich 1990). The original hiring policies at Apple
were similarly unconventional. The belief at The Body Shop was
that the basic skills could be taught, but not the right attitudes and
values (Campbell 1994). In such companies the new hire typically
stays four months or forty years. As one long-term employee of
Marks & Spencer once described it, 'you have to have your
inoculation' and 'if you get a violent reaction, you'd better go'

(Bower and Harris 1991: 348). A further characteristic of many such companies is the value that they place on the employee, and the inclusiveness of their form of capitalism. The 'J & J Credo', at Johnson & Johnson, is typical, placing the company's responsibilities to customers first, employees second, managers third, community fourth, and shareholders fifth and last (Collins and Porras 1991). Lincoln Electric's long-standing policy of fully sharing productivity gains with customers and employees reflects a similar philosophy. As de Pree (1989: 89) put it, 'we who invest our lives in Herman Miller are neither the grist of a corporate mill nor the hired guns of distant, mysterious shareholders', but 'as a faculty and staff are a university, so we are Herman Miller'.

Can corporate culture be the source of sustainable advantage?

While many high-performance companies are characterized by distinctive corporate cultures, the links between culture and competitive advantage are still not fully understood. As Saffold (1988: 546) has argued, the 'strong culture models' of Deal and Kennedy, and others, remain 'intuitively appealing' but tend to 'oversimplify the relationship'. Denison (1984), in one of the earliest empirical tests, did establish a link between participative cultures and performance, but readily acknowledged that this was taking a very narrow view of corporate culture. Later studies, like that of Calori and Sarnin (1991), found that strong culture appeared to be clearly related to firm growth, but the link with profitability was less significant. In sum, the results on the culture–performance relationship remain equivocal, and even the validity of using strength as the most appropriate measure of culture is still open to debate (Saffold 1988).

According to Barney (1986) a firm's culture can only be the source of sustainable competitive advantage under a relatively narrow set of conditions. The culture must be valuable, rare and imperfectly imitable. Prescriptions based on instrumental views of culture (culture as something organizations *have*) 'cannot be used to describe how less successful firms, by modifying their cultures, can come to enjoy sustained superior economic performance' (p. 657). By identifying the more imitable elements of culture, as they tend to do, they can only help the weaker firms to close the performance gap. A more interpretative view of culture (as something organizations *are*) sees the elements that are the true sources of sustainable competitive advantage in organizations as deeply layered in the 'unique circumstances of their founding', the 'unique personalities of their founders' and the 'unique circumstances of their growth', since 'history defies easy imitation' (p. 660). While instrumentalists like O'Reilly (1989: 16) might claim that 'there is nothing magical or elusive about corporate culture', and that norms promoting or impeding desired behaviours can be readily established or changed, Barney (1986) is not so sure (see also Fitzgerald 1988). In his view, firms that have been gifted by history with valuable, rare and inimitable cultures should learn how to appreciate, develop and nurture them in order to sustain their advantage. Firms that have not been so gifted should probably look to sources of competitive advantage other than culture.

While a particular corporate culture may be intrinsically rare and inimitable, its competitive value may be contingent on external factors, and change with time and context. According to O'Reilly (1989) the value of any particular corporate culture will depend on the fit with company strategy. The Honda culture, for example, which remains dedicated to the founding dream of Soichiro to create 'products that are unrivaled in the world', will never be consistent with a low-cost commodity strategy (Honda Annual Report 1991/2). Furthermore, the superior performances of companies like Wal-Mart Stores and Marks & Spencer have been shown to be rooted in the wider congruence among logistical configuration, coordination of material and information flows, culture, and product-market strategy (Leavy 1991a).

The fit between strategy and culture is not the only contingency affecting competitive value. As Saffold (1988) and others have pointed out, organizations are typically characterized by multiple sub-cultures, functional, business and regional, shaped by shared professional, industry and country norms and values (Grinyer and Spender 1979; Calori and Sarnin 1991; Gordon 1991). How they are all interrelated and managed may also have a major impact on firm performance. The relative influence of these different sub-cultures is still difficult to determine. Ohmae (1989b: 143), for example, has little doubt that in a commercial corporation 'commonalities in a business culture are so important to economic success that they easily outweigh traditional differences in language or secular culture'. Others, however, believe that trying to get the relationships right between business cultures and country cultures still remains a formidable strategic challenge (Taylor 1991; Murphy 1994).

POTENTIAL PITFALLS OF 'STRONG' LEADERSHIP AND CULTURE

While value-rich leadership and corporate culture can be very potent sources of superior performance, they have their dangers, dark sides and potential excesses. One of the biggest dangers is what Miller (1990) has called the Icarus paradox: the more successful these leaders and their organizations become, the more invincible they feel and the more resistant to change – which is often the source of their ultimate downfall. What creates such hubris 'remains very much an enigma' (Kets de Vries 1990: 752). How to prevent it from developing can be challenging, and sometimes requires an imaginative response. Schlumberger had its own in-house Columbo, with right of access to any meeting, to help force people to think and prevent the company 'from becoming an establishment' (Auletta 1991: 413). Akio Morita (1986) hired a brash young opera singer to help keep the Sony engineers more fully challenged in their search for high-fidelity products. Strong corporate culture, it has been argued, 'is only overturned with great difficulty', and can too easily lead to 'groupthink and a pressure to conform to the dominant view' (Pfeffer 1992: 42). It can often be the basis for a 'virtuous circle', but if and when 'the alternatives allowed for by the culture' become 'unsuited to new problems', then it can become 'a vicious circle impeding change' (Gagliardi 1986: 117). Likewise, if a charismatic leader's vision becomes suspect, then the same driving conviction that once led a company to greatness can also bring it to the brink of disaster, as happened at Apple and Polaroid (Leavy 1992).

We must also recognize that visionary leaders are not necessarily paragons of either virtue or emotional maturity. Many are narcissistic, obsessive, and the antithesis of the well-rounded, emotionally mature personality that is the implied ideal for the modern manager (Kets de Vries and Miller 1985). For example, it is public knowledge that Ted Turner of CNN has required sustained 'medication and psychiatric counseling' to help stabilize his mood swings (Painton 1992: 29). Former colleagues remember Steve Jobs as someone bordering on 'megalomania' (Butcher 1988: 122), with whom 'the highs were unbelievable but the lows were unimaginable' (Dumaine 1993: 46). Furthermore, we should remember that fear remains a very powerful motivator in organizational life, and an important dimension of charisma (Hopfl 1992). This is evident in Fortune's recent list of America's toughest bosses, which featured such high performance leaders as Edwin 'Prince of Darkness' Artzt of Proctor & Gamble, and John 'Jack the Ripper' Grundhofer of First Bank System (Dumaine 1993: 45–51). It remains true in organizations all over the world that some of the most creative people are stimulated to 'out-of-their-skins' performances by psychologically abusive leaders who mess with their minds and play games with their egos (Dumaine 1993).

Value-rich leadership and culture are very powerful influences, with insidious potential if abused. The charisma associated with both is the third face of power, the power to control definitions of reality and views of the world (Lukes 1974). 'More than other forms of control', as Ray (1986: 287) has warned, 'corporate culture elicits sentiment and emotion, and contains possibilities to ensnare workers in a hegemonic system.' Instrumentalists take a more positive view of culture as a potential form of control. For example, O'Reilly (1989: 12) views it as potentially more satisfying than formal control, because 'we often feel as if we have great autonomy, even though paradoxically we are conforming much more'. Pascale (1985: 27) warns that Western companies will have to learn to reconcile themselves to the 'socialization' inherent in corporate culture, if they are not to 'undermanage the forces for cohesion in organizations'. Can management be trusted with the potential power that strong corporate culture provides? Can culture be the solvent for dissolving most internal political conflict, as the instrumentalists would seem to believe? Radical theorists like Clegg (1990) are not so sure on either count. He reminds us that 'the social construction of reality should never be regarded as a disinterested affair' (p. 143). Even in Japanese companies, which are often taken as models for the West, the historical evidence suggests that the creation of strong organizational culture may be less about collective solidarity and cohesion than 'control from above' (p. 143). Likewise, Hopfl (1992: 29) remains quite sceptical about the 'liberation through submission' promise implicit in charisma and culture, and believes that 'when the power of the corporate definition of reality is diminished – by distance, or drink, or disaster', the 'underlying anxieties, perplexities and conflicts' tend to become apparent.

Finally it should be recognized that strong leadership and culture may have regressive effects on the development of followers as mature individuals, with longer-term implications for psychological health and overall corporate performance (Pauchant 1991). Gemmill and Oakley (1992) have even gone so far as to characterize the notion of charismatic leadership as an 'alienating social myth', that can de-skill followers, both intellectually and emotionally, through the fostering of unhealthy dependency and uncritical devotion. The mutual effect of leaders and followers on each other, and the processes of transference and attribution often involved, will remain important areas for further exploration in future studies of leadership, culture and performance for some time to come (Pauchant 1991).

SUMMARY

In this chapter we examined the relationships between leadership, culture and performance. We began by briefly revisiting some of the attempts in the literature to isolate the essence of leadership effectiveness in attributes and styles. We assessed the importance of specific organizational and industry experience to leadership effectiveness, and reviewed the emergent process view, which focuses on the dynamics of leadership performance in historical context. This more dynamic process view then led us on to examine how effectiveness varies over leadership tenure, an issue that until quite recently had received relatively little research attention in the strategy area. We examined the debate raised by Zaleznik's provocative assertion that managers and leaders are different. We noted the renewed interest in the concept of charismatic leadership and then explored the link between symbol and substance in the relationship between leadership and economic performance. Many people now see the concepts of leadership and strategy as merging into that of strategic vision. We examined the link between vision, values and strategic intent. Considerations of symbols and values led naturally to an exploration of the relationship between leadership and corporate culture, and the process of institutionalizing charisma. We also considered whether culture can be the source of sustainable competitive advantage, contrasting the instrumentalist and interpretative views on this issue. The chapter ended with an examination of some of the pitfalls associated with charisma and strong corporate culture.

Can corporate culture always be managed, as the instrumentalists imply? Or is it more accurate to see it in terms of something that can be sometimes harnessed and shaped, as the more interpretative view would suggest? While only touched on here, this issue is central to any consideration of organizational transformation and renewal, which we go on to examine in the next chapter, as the last of our five key processes.

Chapter 6

Transformation and renewal

During the 1960s and 1970s, the strategy field's preoccupation with growth and diversification was reflected in the popular frameworks of the period, such as portfolio matrices. New business strategies were developed primarily for new businesses. New strategies for existing businesses were less prominent concerns.

Since the early 1980s the emphasis has shifted. Many of the world's leading corporations have had to reassess their basic strategies fundamentally, restructure their corporate portfolios, renew and rejuvenate their core businesses, and even radically reengineer their basic business processes. Driven primarily by the emergence of the new economy, the processes of transformation and renewal have since become among the most central concerns of the strategy field. How difficult is renewal in established companies? What are the main dynamics of the renewal process, and what are the issues and skills involved in its management? These are the themes that will engage us in this chapter, as we examine our fifth and final key process.

STRATEGIC CHANGE – HOW DIFFICULT, AND WHY?

Perspectives on the ease, or frequency, of the process of strategic change vary widely. They range all the way from the firm as continuously adaptable to the firm as totally constrained.

The continuously adaptable corporation and logical incrementalism

One of the most widely used metaphors in the strategy field is the concept of the organization as an open system (Katz and Kahn 1978; Thompson 1967). In this view, companies are in constant interaction with their environments, and the essence of strategy is to achieve the optimum organization–environment fit. The perspective of Goodstein and Burke (1991: 6) is typical: 'Organizations tend to change primarily because of external pressure rather than an internal desire or need for change', and the 'competent organization' can 'promptly move to make internal changes designed to keep it viable in the changing external world'. For many, the concept of the continuously adaptable firm is central to their whole notion of strategic management (Schendel and Hofer 1979; Chakravarthy 1982).

In fact, there are actually two linked processes involved within the adaptation model: the external fit between the firm's strategy and the environment, and the internal fit among the firm's structure, systems and strategy. The original two-stage rational model of the strategy process (formulation–implementation) clearly reflects this perspective. As Ginsberg and Abrahamson (1991: 173) characterize it, this 'rational school of thought' asserts that 'when environmental changes are perceived to have occurred, strategists recognize available strategic options, evaluate them and make the appropriate decisions'. These strategists are also seen to have the administrative skill to bring about swift internal realignment in structures and systems to support the new strategic departures. Miles and Snow (1978) characterized organizations strategically as reactors, defenders, analysers, and prospectors, based on fundamental differences in their overall adaptive capabilities. These categories were seen as progressive, with prospectors coming as close to the notion of the continuously adaptive organization as we are likely to find anywhere in the strategy literature (Miles and Snow 1978; Chakravarthy 1982).

Critics have long since recognized a number of limitations with the original perspective. Due to the finite information processing capabilities of individuals and organizations (Simon 1955, 1956), all firms adapt to their 'perceived' environments with some degree of time-lag and lack of precision (Smircich and Stubbart 1985: 726). Adaptation, therefore, always involves some degree of experimentation and learning. Quinn (1978) offered his model of logical incrementalism as a sensible way for dealing with bounded rationality, and with the political nature of strategic change in most organizations (March 1962; Pettigrew 1977; Murray 1978; Narayanan and Fahey 1982). He saw strategic change as an incremental 'continuous, evolving, political, consensus building process with neither a finite beginning nor end' (Quinn 1982: 623).

Some have suggested that logical incrementalism is not really a strategic perspective on change, but merely a reactive one. Quinn has rejected this criticism, and argued that, in the hands of skilful executives, the process of logical incrementalism was seen to be a 'purposeful, powerful management technique for integrating the analytical, behavioural, political and timing aspects of strategy formulation' (p. 614). It was a view of process later echoed in the work of those who tended to see strategies as created over time in a crafted but not fully preformulated fashion, rather than as point-in-time plans that are periodically reviewed and adjusted (Kotter 1982; Mintzberg 1987). Indeed the underlying notion that purposeful strategists 'try to build a resource base', so 'strong and flexible that the enterprise can survive and prosper towards its vision despite all but the most devastating events' (Quinn 1982: 613), also finds many resonances in more recent resource-based theory (Wernerfelt 1984; Conner 1991; Mahoney and Pandian 1992; Wiersema and Hansen 1993). It is in tune with the growing belief that the primary bases for successful strategies in today's dynamic environment are core competencies rather than product-market positions (Prahalad and Hamel 1990).

The notion that organizations are perpetually adaptable continues to command strong support. For example, the Organization Development literature, which has made a 'prolific contribution to theories of organization change', generally presents an 'ideology of gradualism' (Dunphy and Stace 1988: 317). Furthermore a central objective of the widely influential total quality management (TQM) and just-in-time (JIT) approaches is to institutionalize the process of continuous improvement, or relentless incremental change, as a way of life (Schaffer and Thompson 1992). These approaches are about developing the capability to 'get your adaptation in first' (to paraphrase a popular cliché), and in this way to maintain strategic control over your company's destiny. A story from Honda provides an interesting illustration. In 1985, the Accord was listed among the ten best cars sold in America by *Car and Driver*, for the third consecutive year. The feature writer declared that there was 'nothing wrong with the Honda Accord. Nothing.' Yet in the same year the company made a full model change and, as former President Irmajiri later recalled, 'changed everything'. Why? Because 'we believed we could make it better' (Pearson and Ehrlich 1990: 4).

Explanations differ quite widely on the motive forces driving the adaptation process. Many see the external environment as the primary driver. The organization's continuing need to reduce uncertainty (Thompson 1967 – open systems theory), maintain external legitimacy (Meyer and Rowan 1977 – institutional theory), and reduce resource dependency (Pfeffer and Salancik 1978 – resource dependence theory) have all been mooted. On the other hand the incrementalist, organizational learning, organizational development and TQM/JIT perspectives have all tended to emphasize strategic intent (Quinn 1978; March 1981; Beckhard and Harris 1987; Schaffer and Thompson 1992). These differences notwithstanding, the notion of the continuously adaptable corporation has been 'the dominant perspective in the study of organizations' (Singh *et al.* 1986: 587), and remains a very powerful one within the strategy field.

The strategically inflexible corporation – psychology, ecology and ideology

In spite of its power and prevalence, however, the notion of the continuously adaptable corporation is far from universally shared. A number of perspectives emphasize the forces for continuity and inertia that tend to develop in organizational settings, posing serious questions about the capacity of any organization to adapt readily. According to Miller and Friesen (1980: 591), 'the one theme that stands out in the literature is that organizations tend to demonstrate great sluggishness in adapting', even 'when their environments threaten them with extinction'.

Several authors have emphasized the role of history in circumscribing an organization's scope for future change (Greiner 1972; Kimberly 1979; Boeker 1989). For example, Greiner (1972: 38) argued that a firm's future 'may be less determined by outside forces than it is by the organization's history', and its structure 'less malleable' than strategy–structure theorists like Chandler had traditionally assumed. In Kimberly's organizational life cycle perspective, the determining effects of early history were seen in terms somewhat analogous to human development (Kimberly 1979). The overall implication, as Boeker (1989: 492) put it, is that 'early patterns of organizing may limit the range of strategic actions that firms are likely to consider'. For example, the internal hub-and-spoke, cross-docking logistics system that was developed over the years by Wal-Mart Stores has become one of the company's enduring sources of competitive advantage, according to Stalk *et al.* (1992). Yet this 'core capability' did not originally emerge from any unique strategic insight into the industry, or deliberate attempt to change the existing rules of the game. Rather, Wal-Mart developed it out of historical necessity, when it became clear that the main independent distributors of the time were uninterested in servicing the needs of an emerging discount chain, concentrated in small population centres. It has since become such an integral part of Wal-Mart's overall strategic posture, however, that is difficult to imagine the company ever significantly departing from it, whatever the future pressures for change.

Other perspectives have emphasized further constraints on change. For example, Staw (1976) has shown that individuals and groups have strong psychological tendencies to increase their commitment to a given strategy, even when negative consequences indicate the need for change. The Lockheed L 1011 Tri-Star Jet programme is a classic example (Staw and Ross 1987). Several explanations have been offered, ranging from the 'gambler's fallacy' (sooner or later the odds must turn) to a strong desire to avoid the appearance of weakness, often associated with 'U-turns', particularly in Western culture (Staw 1976; Staw and Ross 1987). On the other hand, organizations with a long history of success can become over-confident, inward-looking and resistant to change (Kets de Vries 1990; Miller 1990). The slow responses of Coca-Cola to the Pepsi challenge of the late 1960s and IBM to the new competition in the computer industry during the 1980s are classic examples. Even when companies want to change strategy, they can face significant barriers to mobility in their wider industry structures (Porter 1980, 1981). This was dramatically illustrated by the inability of the resourceful Philip Morris Corporation to reposition 7-Up from niche player to industry leader in the soft drink industry of the 1980s.

One of the main perspectives that questions the notion of the continuously adaptive corporation is the population ecology model. Hannan and Freeman (1977) argued that adaptation to environmental change happens primarily at the level of organizational populations rather than individual firms. Industries tend to be adaptive; organizations tend to be relatively inert. A dramatic illustration is the recent 'deconstruction' of the computer industry, which saw the once-dominant, vertically integrated giants like IBM and Digital being unseated by relatively new arrivals like Sun Microsystems, Dell and Microsoft (Verity 1992). Such radical structural changes at industry population level are not new. Aldrich (1979), for example, has shown that during the 1940s and 1950s some 3 million new firms were created in the United States and almost the same number discontinued. Industry renewal, according to the population ecology perspective, takes place largely through selection processes analogous to Darwinism. As Hannan and Freeman (1984: 150) put it, 'population ecology theory holds that most of the variability in organizational structures comes about through the creation of new organizations and organizational forms and the replacement of old ones'. It may be that, no matter how hard we try to help organizations to become masters of change, the process of adaptation at industry level will always involve a high degree of decay and rebirth at the level of the firm.

The population ecologists highlight the importance of inertial forces, such as specialized assets and skills, internal political pressures, or external legitimation processes, that tend to inhibit adaptation (Hannan and Freeman 1977). More importantly, they take issue with the widely held assumption, underpinning the open systems model, that selection processes invariably favour adaptable forms of life. In fact they argue that selection processes 'tend to favour organizations whose structure is difficult to change' (Hannan and Freeman 1984: 149). It is reliability and accountability that tend to give the established organization ecological durability over newer, more *ad hoc* and organic forms, rather than technical advantage (the 'no-one ever got fired for buying IBM or hiring Caterpillar' effect, which sustained the commercial leadership of these companies long after their technical advantages had been eroded). The dilemma at the heart of the ecological view is that 'the capacity to reproduce a structure with high fidelity' is seen as a prerequisite for reliable and accountable performance, and the price to be paid for this is 'structural inertia' (Hannan and Freeman 1984: 162). Structurally stable organizations have better survival prospects than more fluid forms in the medium term; neither have great survival prospects in the longer term, unless the environment remains quite stable. It is the relative inertia of organizations that ultimately determines whether radically new phases in industry evolution will be dominated by new arrivals or transformed incumbents. 'Other things being equal, the faster the speed with which new organizations can be built, the greater is the (relative) inertia of a set of existing structures', and the greater the threat to the incumbents (Hannan and Freeman 1984: 152).

The ideological or paradigmatic perspective also seriously questions the ability of organizations to adapt continuously (Sheldon 1980; Brunsson 1982; Starbuck 1982; Pettigrew 1987; Johnson 1988). This interpretative view of continuity and change is rooted in the cognitive, political and cultural processes of organizational life, and in an enacted model of organization–environment interaction. The external environment is seen not as a neatly packaged 'out-there' objective reality to be perceived and reacted to, but as 'an ambiguous field of experience' that has to be interpreted into sense-making patterns by organizational strategists (Smircich and Stubbart 1985: 726). The interpreted environment (and not just the perceived environment) becomes the foundation for organizational action. The effects of this enacted view can be seen in the widely shared beliefs and strategic recipes that typically operate at industry level (Grinyer and Spender 1979). To recall some examples from an earlier chapter, in the US retailing industry during the 1970s, it was widely believed that discount stores were not economically viable in population centres of fewer than 100,000 people. As a result, Wal-Mart stores, with a different interpretation, enjoyed an almost non-contested ten-year opportunity before this commonly held belief was radically altered. Bic in ball-point pens and Head in metal skis are other examples of companies that found significant opportunities through operating within a different interpreted environment from the rest of their industries.

These shared interpretations also develop at organizational level, and can be extremely resistant to revision. According to Sheldon (1980: 62), 'all organizations tend toward a paradigm – toward some perfect fit reflecting some idealized way of working which is cherished'. Such paradigms provide a sense of shared certainty in the face of ambiguity, a stable resolution of political interests, and simply valued traditions. As Johnson (1988: 85) put it, the paradigm 'is not just a system of core beliefs', but is 'preserved and legitimized in a cultural web of organizational action in terms of myths, rituals, symbols, control systems and formal and informal power structures which support and provide relevance to the core beliefs'. Others prefer to talk about organizational ideologies, when discussing these widely shared world views (Meyer 1982). Brunsson (1982: 38) believes that such ideologies 'tend to arise by themselves in organizations', but recognizes that they can also be 'consciously moulded' by key actors and groups. Pettigrew (1987: 659) also points out that they tend to provide cultural legitimacy for 'unobtrusive systems of power', with powerful interests vested in their ongoing conservation. For whatever reasons, such paradigms or ideologies can often become ultrastable. The organizations concerned become 'unable to adapt and learn', resisting any information they receive that implies failure or the need for radical change, 'because acceptance would destroy their stability' (Sheldon 1980: 62).

CYCLES OF CHANGE

Organizations, it would seem, continually experience significant forces for change and continuity. How these forces get resolved remains one of the central concerns of all those interested in the processes of strategic change and transformation.

Evolutionary and revolutionary cycles of change

Strategic change is now seen by many to be cyclical, characterized by long periods of evolutionary change interspersed with shorter episodes of more radical transformation (Greiner 1972; Miller and Friesen 1980; Pettigrew 1985; Tushman *et al.* 1986; Mintzberg 1987; Johnson 1990). This kind of 'punctuated equilibrium model' has applications in many fields (Gersick 1991). In the strategy field, some see the cyclical pattern in terms of fit and functionality while others see it as a historical process.

Tushman *et al.* (1986: 39) see the long evolutionary periods of convergence as 'profoundly functional', allowing a company to 'build on its strengths' and to finesse them through continuous incremental improvements and consolidations. Frame-breaking change, on the other hand, is seen as 'quite dysfunctional when the organization is successful'. When such changes do become necessary, as a result of industry discontinuities or product life-cycle shifts, 'the more rapidly they are implemented, the more quickly the organization can reap the benefits of the following convergent period'. In a similar vein, Miller (1982: 132) has argued that 'the functional aspects of resistance to change' have been generally ignored in organizational studies, and the desirability of piecemeal and incremental change overemphasized. For Miller, the ideal fit among strategy, structure and environment involves a consistent configuration. Within-configuration adjustments can be easily accommodated, but between-configuration transitions will be resisted for sound functional reasons until the case becomes almost overwhelming. However, he could also see the potential for dysfunctionality in the cyclical pattern. The evolutionary phase can 'forestall expensive reversals' and avoid 'hair-trigger adaptiveness', but it can also lead to a deterioration in performance as a result of 'sluggish adaptation' (Miller and Friesen 1980: 611). In the other phase, many revolutions do bring renewal, but some can 'reverse a perfectly good strategy or structure', because of overreaction or over-zealousness, and many of these costly transformations 'never pay off' (p. 611).

In contrast, Pettigrew (1985, 1987) and Johnson (1988, 1990) have tended to focus on the political, cultural and historical nature of the process, in their explanations for the punctuated pattern. According to Johnson (1988), for example, a strategy of logical incrementalism often fails to keep pace with environmental change, because of the conservative political and cultural drag associated with a stable paradigm. This usually leads to 'strategic drift', which eventually necessitates a burst of radical readjustment to bring the organization and its environment back into alignment. This pattern is not so much functional as historically inevitable, owing to the complex social nature of most organizations.

TRANSFORMATION AND RENEWAL – PROCESS DYNAMICS

Given that there are always strong forces for continuity in organizations, how do major strategic transformations come about? One of the most popular perspectives is the classic Lewin (1951) unfreeze–change–refreeze model. Many of the later models are variations on this multi-phase view (Goodstein and Burke 1991; Stopford and Baden-Fuller 1990; Johnson 1990; Antonioni 1994; Strebel 1994). Some stress the importance of 'unlearning', double-loop learning, and the renewal of shared mental models, in radical organizational change (Argyris and Schon 1978; Starbuck 1982; Nystrom and Starbuck 1984; Barr *et al.* 1992). Others see the revolutionary change process mainly in terms of fundamental revisions in organizational ideologies, paradigms or archetypes (Pettigrew 1987; Child and Smith 1987; Greenwood and Hinings 1988; Johnson 1988; Stopford and Baden-Fuller 1990; Gersick 1991). Most see the process of transformation involving destruction and reconstruction. As Nonaka (1988a: 57) succinctly put it, the 'self-renewal of an organization can be seen as a process of dissolving an existing organizational order and creating a new one'. The entire process typically takes time, and represents a period of uncertainty, dissonance, heightened political tension and general organizational discomfort. How do such processes start, how are they played out, and how are they strategically managed?

There are, as yet, no definitive models (beyond the basic unfreeze–change–refreeze framework), and different authors have tended to emphasize different aspects of the process. As Johnson (1990: 187) observed, there is 'a developing but still unclear picture', and further research is 'sorely needed' (Hoffman 1989: 65). However, certain themes recur. Most agree on the emergent/learning nature of the process, and on the importance of momentum, critical mass, leadership and crisis as key elements in the determination of direction, pace and ultimate success. To overcome the forces for continuity, a momentum for change must develop. This is usually seen as a cumulative process, often fed in its early stages by a number of semi-autonomous developments that begin to challenge and erode the status quo. Momentum building often involves political and cultural action, because of the different rationalities operating across the different levels and interests in the organization (Tichy and Devanna 1986; Child and Smith 1987; Leavy 1991b). As Pettigrew (1987: 659) so aptly put it, transformation is 'ultimately a product of a legitimation process shaped by political/cultural considerations, though often expressed in rational/analytical terms'. If the transformation is to be ultimately successful this momentum must reach a critical mass, beyond which it tends to generate its own self-sustaining dynamic (Pettigrew 1987; Child and Smith 1987; Leavy 1991b).

Few have difficulty with the foregoing as an overall model of process. Where views tend to differ are on questions like: where does the initial momentum come from, and how does it typically build up? What role does an experimental/learning approach play? Can such a process be managed strategically, and if so how? How important a stimulus is crisis and/or a change of leadership to the success of the transformation? These are the kinds of question that will engage us for the remainder of the chapter.

The emergent nature of the process

The seeds of transformation are often sown within organizations long before the process becomes highly visible and deliberately managed. This emergent nature was a common feature in the transformations at Cadbury, ICI and Ford during the 1970s and 1980s. At Cadbury, the process 'passed through several stages', with no clear beginning or end (Child and Smith 1987: 591). At Ford it 'involved a confluence of initiatives undertaken at every level of the organization', but 'no master plan' (Schlesinger et al. 1990: 5-6). There was no master plan either at ICI (Pettigrew 1987). 'Innovation in emergent strategies' was seen as 'critical' to successful rejuvenation, in the cases studied by Stopford and Baden-Fuller (1990: 399). As Kanter (1991: 8–9) put it, 'organizations seeking total transformation cannot avoid the messy, mistake-ridden muddling stage', and retrospective accounts often neglect to describe 'how much trial and error was involved'. In many ways, some have argued, transformation and renewal should be seen as an innovation process, and managed accordingly (Nonaka 1988a; Chew et al. 1991). The key innovations and initiatives are often those of middle management (Kanter 1982; Nonaka 1988b).

The reasons why such processes tend to be more emergent than deliberate are partly cognitive, partly political and partly cultural. Even where visions for change were developed, they tended to remain necessarily vague and ambiguous in the early stages of transformation, and only became more fully developed, and widely accepted, after extended phases of experimentation and legitimation (Pettigrew 1987; Nonaka 1988a; Stopford and Baden-Fuller 1990). As Child and Smith (1987: 590) put it, the 'wide acceptance and cohesion' provided by 'the traditional and hitherto dominant ideology' often 'provided a clear position against which the case for change had to be developed'. In AT&T, for example, the traditional inward-looking engineering mind-set had to be replaced with a more market-oriented ideology. The organization had to be convinced that 'Mother Bell' didn't live there anymore (Kennedy 1989). At Ford, successful transformation required the erosion of the traditional finance-dominated mind-set and functional parochialism, before significant renewal was possible.

Managing the process – building momentum

The strategic management of transformation requires the 'patience' to persevere with the long-term 'conditioning' process of challenging the ideology that was 'nurtured' in an earlier era (Pettigrew 1987: 667). It requires the subtle ability to do this while recognizing that renewal must be ultimately brought about through metamorphosis of the old ideology, not through its total destruction. It demands an intellectual and intuitive understanding of the configuration among interpretative schemata, socio-political processes and structural attributes that is the essence of the internally consistent paradigm or archetype (Greenwood and Hinings 1988). Successful renewal also requires a leadership that is willing to pursue bold new strategic initiatives, while trying to stimulate and harness this emergent process (Hoffman 1989; Stopford and Baden-Fuller 1990; Robbins and Pearce 1992). For example, the willingness of Jan Carlzon at SAS to invest in a new strategy to reposition the company as the 'businessman's airline', at a time of mounting losses, was vital to the company's turnaround (Ghoshal 1989). Similarly, the willingness of the Petersen–Poling leadership to invest in the highly innovative, bet-the-company Taurus project, when the traditional ideology was pointing to retrenchment, was critical to Ford's renewal during the 1982–9 period (Schlesinger *et al.* 1990).

Autonomous initiatives of various kinds tend to arise in most organizations as part of ongoing activity (Bower 1970; Burgleman 1983a; Kanter 1983). The leadership of transformation involves, among other things, the ability to nurture selectively those initiatives with renewal potential, which can help subvert the old ideology and open the organization up further to the possibility of change. Undermining the existing paradigm or ideology can also involve the selective use (even leaking) of plans and reports to foster discontent with the status quo, as happened, for example, in both ICI and the Burton Group during the 1970s (Pettigrew 1985; Johnson 1990). It can further involve highly dramatic and symbolic acts, like the burning of old records at Marks & Spencer during the overhead reduction campaign of the 1950s, the massive dumping of the old product line to signal a fundamental shift in product policy at Asaki Breweries, Iacocca's famous personal salary cut to $1 a year at Chrysler, or AT&T's move from its 'wonderful old classic' headquarters at 195 Broadway, to underline forcefully the break with the past (Tunstall 1986: 115).

As with reforming movements generally, the renewal process in organizations is often a contest between small numbers of conservative and reforming activists for the hearts and minds of the less committed majority. Building momentum to critical mass does not usually require the complete conversion of the greater number. It involves unearthing key activists and finding ways to empower them. You don't need many. 'Give me 40 people', as Jack Sparks of Whirlpool once declared, 'and I can run this company' (Tichy and Devanna 1986: 193). But as Mike Walsh of Tenneco points out, you have to 'pick those with a burning desire for change', and they are often 'buried down the organization' (Sherman 1993: 44). Sometimes it involves the patient management of every opportunity to move the change agenda forward, 'waiting for people to retire to exploit any policy vacuum created' or 'backing off and waiting or moving the pressure point for change', as required to keep momentum going (Pettigrew 1987: 667). Sometimes it can be accelerated by replacing many of the most prominent guardians of the old ideology, as Iacocca did at Chrysler and Carlzon at SAS. It can also be promoted in other ways. AT&T used strategic alliances to help import new ideas and accelerate the demise of the old ideology (Kennedy 1989). Ford, AT&T and SAS all used extensive training programmes for a similar purpose.

The success of the momentum-building phase can hinge on the outcome of certain key defining episodes or projects, and transformational leaders do not need to orchestrate the entire process with equal intensity, if they know how to recognize and leverage them. These are moments of truth when new ideas and values are tested in a very visible way, which amplifies or attenuates the momentum for change as a consequence. The most defining episode in the transformation at Ford was the Taurus project, which was widely recognized as pivotal to the financial and market turnaround of the company. It was a project in which the future face of Ford, whether fundamentally new or marginally adjusted, was always going to be clearly visible. In the event the new processes (employee involvement, concurrent engineering, outward-looking benchmarking, cross-functional cooperation) and new values of the company were given very concrete expression in the Taurus project, which then became an engine for transformation throughout the rest of the company. Likewise, the Chirk factory project, a distinct 'break with embedded Bournville practice', became a defining element in the transformation at Cadbury (Child and Smith 1987: 582).

Is crisis a necessary trigger?

A recurring theme in the literature is the crucial part played by crisis in triggering the process (Starbuck *et al.* 1978; Kanter 1983; Child and Smith 1987; Pettigrew 1987; Nonaka 1988a; Grinyer and McKiernan 1990; Johnson 1990; Stopford and Baden-Fuller 1990). For example, the 'crisis mentality', or 'shared sense of impending disaster', was cited as a major 'catalyst' in the transformation process at Ford, and helped a lot of people to get 'religion' (Schlesinger *et al.* 1990: 5). Likewise the sense of crisis at SAS, heightened by the arrival of Carlzon, and his almost total turnover of top management, helped to generate the momentum for change. However, the rapid success of the initial phase, in the SAS case, then actually diminished this momentum, and threatened to undermine the ultimate transformation of the company (Ghoshal 1989). Discontinuities, like deregulation, technological breakthrough or foreign competition, are often sources of externally induced crises. However, there is strong evidence to suggest that many, if not most, of the crises leading to turnaround result from internal errors of omission and commission (Hoffman 1989). At AT&T, for example, the company could have 'detected the shape of its future as early as 1968', and had several later chances to prepare in a more gradual way for the transformation that took place during the 1980s. However, the old culture resisted the signals until they became shock waves. Likewise, the developments that led to the dramatic downturn in performance at Ford, in the late 1970s, had been discernible well in advance of the eventual crisis. Overall, as Pettigrew (1987: 665) put it, transformation seems to require crisis, because in non-crisis conditions even the most senior advocates of change often 'do not have sufficient

leverage to break through the pattern of inertia in their organizations'.

In sum, it seems that periodic crises may be necessary
precursors for organizational renewal. However, it is one of the
ironies of organizational life that 'the processes which produce
crises are substantially identical with the processes which produce
successes' (Starbuck *et al.* 1978: 114; see also Miller 1990). If so, is
there anything to be gained, other than forced transformation,
from such episodes? Starbuck *et al.* (1978) remind us that the
Chinese ideogram for crisis combines the symbols for danger and
opportunity. Similarly, Meyer (1982: 59) points out that 'when
adversity looms', astute strategists should be alert for the
'clandestine opportunities', presented by the crisis-induced flux,
to achieve some long-cherished objectives that were unrealizable
otherwise. Furthermore, as Jack Welch of General Electric
suggests, 'managing in a difficult environment' tends to 'train
you a hell of a lot better than riding the wave of success' (Sherman
1993: 41). Strategists can also use the learning opportunities
presented by crisis to temper the steel of their organizations for the
challenges that lie beyond recovery and renewal.

Is new leadership normally needed?

Can current leaders successfully manage the transformation of
their companies? The evidence suggests that it is unlikely.
Hoffman (1989) reports that leadership change is very common
during the early stages of turnaround, and O'Neill (1986) has
shown that in successful turnarounds the top manager is almost
twice as likely to be replaced by an outsider as an insider. The
reasons for this are both substantive and symbolic (Hoffman 1989;
Leavy 1995). Very often the situation reaches crisis because
existing leaders attempt to rationalize unfolding events to fit with
the existing strategy and organizational paradigm, on which they
have probably built their careers. As Starbuck *et al.* (1978: 120) so
colourfully put it, such leaders continue to live in 'collapsing
palaces', trying to preserve the internal harmony of their once-
elegant creations, while the mountain-tops that they rest on are
'crumbling from erosion'. The conservative reaction of the existing
leadership eventually leads to loss of credibility arising out of
declining performance, which, along with its attachment to the old
order, undermines its capacity to lead the renewal process.

Furthermore, the symbolism associated with the arrival of a new leader can also facilitate renewal, through heightening the sense of crisis and conditioning the organization for radical change (Leavy 1995). In addition, crises provide the kind of context likely to give rise to an eruption of charismatic devotion (Westley and Mintzberg 1989; Bryman 1993). This is most likely to attach itself to a new leader (already cast in the role of potential saviour), and may also prove very functional in the overall achievement of successful transformation.

CAN THE CYCLICAL PATTERN BE BROKEN?

Are there any indications that organizations can find ways to break the punctuated equilibrium pattern or at least better mitigate its potentially destructive effects? Must thousands of people continue to have their lives so painfully disrupted in the massive restructurings that have been typically associated with such cyclical patterns to date? These are questions that will continue to engage us well into the new century.

The punctuated pattern at organizational level mirrors similar patterns at the levels of industries and economies (Meyer *et al.* 1990; Beck 1992). Economic renewal has always involved the death of some industries and the birth of others; industry renewal, the death of some organizations and the birth of others; and organizational renewal, the death of some business units and the birth of others. It is difficult to see this pattern changing radically in the foreseeable future. It is now generally recognized that we are in the midst of revolutionary change at world economy level – a process of change similar in historical significance to the industrial revolution, with downstream second-order effects to come that we can still barely imagine (Stewart 1993). Have we entered a totally new era of indefinite disequilibrium, or are we on a lengthy transition to a new equilibrium in the international economy? Either way, most of today's strategists at organizational level are likely to be managing in disequilibrium conditions for the rest of their tenures. In such conditions the change cycle at organization level is compressed. Many organizations are on an accelerated roller-coaster ride through the evolutionary–revolutionary change cycle. Can they cope, or must the death–birth pattern intensify, at organizational and business unit levels?

Two processes at the heart of renewal, at whatever level we

view it, are new ideas and the reorganization of resources to exploit them. A number of emergent perspectives seek to offer ways to make renewal a more continuous and less disruptive process. Some see the knowledge-creating process in organizations as the key (Senge 1990a, 1993; Nonaka 1988a, 1994; Brown 1991). They emphasize the importance of learning through aspiration (generative learning), not just adaptation (problem-solving). According to Senge and Nonaka, a key capacity in truly learning organizations is the ability to generate aspirational crises (creative tension/creative crisis) as stimulants to renewal. As Nonaka (1988a: 67) put it, 'setting a high, challenging target is one of the means of self-transcendence'. These ideas are strongly echoed in the Hamel and Prahalad (1989) conceptualization of strategic intent. Furthermore, many of those who believe that disequilibrium is here to stay see potential for a new perspective on renewal in chaos theory, the emergent 'science of process rather than state' (Stevenson and Harmeling 1990: 3).

Others see the potential for continual, or at least less disruptive, renewal in new perspectives on structure. Many believe that the growing preponderance of the network (alliances, supplier partnerships, etc.) in the new economy will herald less disruptive renewal at all levels. Networks potentially generate and circulate knowledge, and challenge internal perspectives, more efficiently than the equivalent array of resources organized into more traditional monolithic hierarchies. As structures, they can also dissolve and reform (absorb creative destruction) with much less social disruption. In a similar way, more flexible structures are also emerging within firms, enhancing their potential for coping with the creative destruction that comes with self-renewal (Bahrami 1992; Ostroff and Smith 1992). Characterized by a new emphasis on process, and facilitated by recent developments in information technologies (Hammer 1990; Hammer and Champy 1993; Teng *et al.* 1994), these new internal arrangements are more effective knowledge-generators and change-absorbers than the more traditional functional hierarchies that they are increasingly replacing.

These are all promising developments. However, we should remain sanguine about their ultimate impact on the cycles of change pattern. We already noted the scepticism about the more transcendent view of the learning organization in an earlier chapter. Even in organizations attempting to implement the very pragmatic philosophy of continuous improvement, there is recent evidence to suggest that the pattern of change is one of punctuated equilibrium (Tyre and Orlikowski 1994). Miles and Snow (1992) remind us that only time will tell whether the network organization will be less prone to internally generated failures than the traditional hierarchy. Business process reengineering (BPR) is proving itself to be an effective, though often painful and hazardous, programme for organizational transformation (Watkins *et al.* 1993; Teng *et al.* 1994). Whether it will turn out to be a once-off, technology-triggered revolution for most firms or can be institutionalized as a capacity for ongoing renewal is still very open to question, as even Hammer and Champy (1993) would readily admit. There is as yet no clear sign that the punctuated pattern will be broken, and disruptive renewal ('for the corporation to live, it must be willing to see business units die' – Bower and Christensen 1995: 53) seems likely to remain a major theme in the strategy field for quite some time.

SUMMARY

In this chapter we examined the processes of transformation and renewal, which are being experienced by more and more companies in the current dynamic and volatile economy. There are two opposing traditions in the literature: one that sees the company as continuously adaptable and the other that sees it as relatively inflexible. The first tradition is reflected in the logical incrementalism, continuous improvement, and open systems views of organizations. The second is informed by diverse perspectives drawn from organizational psychology, population ecology theory and the corporate culture (paradigm/ideology) literature. These two traditions are partially resolved in the punctuated equilibrium or cycles of change (evolutionary–revolutionary) perspective, which has become very influential in the strategy field.

We then explored the dynamics of transformation. There is still no definitive model, but most perspectives to date are variations on Lewin's three-phase unfreeze–change–refreeze view. We examined key aspects of transformation (emergent nature, building momentum, critical mass, defining episodes), in terms of their implications for the successful management of the process. We noted the prevalence of crisis as a trigger for transformation, and the frequency with which new leaders are brought in to manage it, and we considered why these patterns were so common. The chapter ended with a discussion on whether the often disruptive cycles of change pattern can be broken, or its effects greatly mitigated, and an assessment of the likely impact of some current developments (learning organization, networks, business process reengineering) that appear to many to offer hope in this regard.

Having now discussed the last of our five key processes, in the final chapter we shall conclude with some overall reflections.

Chapter 7

Key processes – final reflections

The idea for an examination of key processes in strategy, emphasizing themes and theories, was a reflection of the eclectic nature of the subject, and the plurality of perspectives that have sought to inform it. Strategy, as yet, does not have a paradigm. The most common denominator among the diverse contributors to the field has been a concern with understanding sustainable competitive advantage. Throughout this book the emphasis has been on an examination of some of the 'softer' variables in the strategy process, and their links with hard economic performance. In this final chapter we look back over the terrain covered. The integration of a diverse body of literature, and range of perspectives, under five major topics, has proved to be a challenging task in itself, and no integrative framework is attempted. Yet some overall reflections are appropriate to round off the analysis. Two stand out. One is the degree of interplay among the five processes, and the other is the strong duality at the heart of strategy, most evident when the foregoing analysis as a whole is reviewed in historical perspective. These will be the two main themes of this concluding chapter.

CROSS-CURRENTS AMONG THE PROCESSES

The conceptual framework for this book (illustrated in Figure 1 on page 6) was developed out of my prior research and teaching experience. The prospect of trying to understand each of the five key processes, and their links with sustainable competitive advantage, appeared to offer a fruitful route to a more complete understanding of strategy. I hope the reader by now agrees. I recognized at the outset the interrelatedness of the processes, and expected to find a degree of cross-current among them. What surprised me, as I completed the process-by-process examination, was just how strong some of these cross-currents really were.

The most obvious case was learning. It was seen to have very strong links with all the other processes, lending further support to those in the practical world who believe that the notion of learning will be pivotal to competitiveness in the future (Stata 1989), and also to those who see in it real potential as the unit of analysis (in preference to decision-making) for a more dynamic theory of strategy (Dodgson 1993). We saw learning relate to innovation through the notions of competency (enhancing or destroying), absorptive capacity and creative imitation. The relationship of learning to competitiveness featured as a major rationale for many of the advantages claimed for networks (partnerships and alliances) over traditional, more vertically integrated hierarchies, in the structuring and relationship-patterning area. Learning also featured quite prominently in our discussion of transformation and renewal. Indeed the cycles-of-change model could also be seen in terms of long periods of evolutionary (within paradigm/ single-loop) learning punctuated by shorter bursts of the more revolutionary (trans-paradigm/double-loop) kind. The notion of learning was also to be found in the process view of leadership, and is inherent in the notion of corporate culture.

Learning may have been the most obvious case, but it was clearly not the only one. The notions of innovation and renewal were clearly seen to be related, and it was argued that in many ways the strategic management of transformation and innovation require similar process skills (one emphasizing management innovation, the other product and process innovation). Both are linked by the capacities of product and process innovation to be defining elements in the wider process of organizational transformation. Leadership and culture were also seen to be central to any analysis of the renewal and transformation process. Culture was seen to be a powerful force for continuity (dominant ideology/organizational paradigm), and the symbolism associated with leadership change a dramatic cultural force for wider transformation. The new interest being shown by diversified corporations in federalism promises to link the processes of leadership and structuring in the strategy field even more closely, because federalism is a philosophy to be lived, not just a hierarchy to be administered.

STRATEGY'S DUALITY – ITS RATIONAL AND ROMANTIC NATURE

When we reflect back on the analysis as a whole, we can also find a very strong historical pattern. Many of the traditional perspectives on the key processes tended to be strongly rational-instrumental in character, whereas many of the later themes and theories seemed to reflect the more recent infusion of a strong humanist-interpretative influence.

Up to now we have tended to see these two aspects of strategy as largely competing views. This was evident in the recurring tension that we found between the instrumentalist and interpretative approaches in many of the chapters. It is also evident, more generally, in the recent debate between Ansoff (1991, 1994) and Mintzberg (1990, 1991b, 1994b). This either-or perspective has mainly been a historical legacy. Using a Mr Spock/Captain Kirk, Star Trek metaphor (see Figure 2), a final reprise of our earlier analysis will show that the strategy field developed its own highly rationalist, Spock-like dominant ideology during the first two decades. This was then progressively challenged, and almost totally undermined, by the emergence of a more romantic and adventurous Kirk-type ideology, during the 1980s and early 1990s (in a fashion reminiscent of our portrayal of the transformation and renewal process in Chapter 6). Our reprise will also

Mr Spock (1960s/1970s) *(Rational-Instrumental)*	Captain Kirk (1980s/1990s) *(Romantic-Interpretative)*
Managing	Leading
Scientist/Technologist	Humanist/Philosopher
Generic	Idiosyncratic
Commanding/Controlling	Inspiring/Empowering
Securing conformity	Harnessing diversity
Adaptive	Inventive
Objectives/Instrumental	Purpose/Institutional
Structure/Systems	Culture/Processes
Decision-making/Positioning	Learning/Leveraging
Strategy as problem-solving	Strategy as potential-fulfilling
Strategy as planning	Strategy as crafting
Strategy as prose	Strategy as poetry
(Ansoff)	(Mintzberg)

Figure 2 The duality of strategic management – the Spock–Kirk metaphor

demonstrate why the field should be wary of uncritically embracing this emergent Kirk-type ideology as its dominant new face, and why it should now try to move on beyond the either-or dialectic. It is time to recognize that strategy has both a rational and a romantic nature (see Ebers 1985 for a more philosophical development of the rational–romantic distinction), and to come to terms with this complex duality in our future teaching, research and practice (Leavy 1995b).

The Spock era – the first two decades

A consistent theme, across the processes, was the predominance of the rational-instrumental view of strategy during the 1960s and 1970s. This was the era when the Spock side of strategy was in the ascendant. It was a period in which the modern corporation was seen as the major instrument of social and economic progress in most developed countries. Organization, rather than individual flair, was felt to be the crucial determinant of long-run success, and business schools were being founded in the expectation that management could be developed as a science. While charismatic entrepreneurs were often seen to be involved in the foundation of enterprises, a company's future was only felt to be secured when it successfully completed the transition to professional 'scientific' management. The dominant metaphor for the organization itself was the efficient machine. Each part was replaceable, even the top leadership, with minimum disruption to its overall functioning. This picture was graphically captured by a contemporary feature in the *New Republic* magazine, which described the professional manager of the times in the following way:

> He plans, organizes and controls large enterprises in a calm, logical, dispassionate and decisive manner. The symbols in which he thinks and works are those of finance, law, accounting and psychology. Finessed and massaged into ever new formulations they yield wondrous abstractions. And because the professional manager deals in abstractions, he can move from company to company with relative ease, manipulating people and capital as he goes. Without any abiding commitment to the company, he is the master of the quick fix, yielding the sort of short-term profits that institutional investors love.
>
> (Kotter 1982: 131)

The notion of strategic planning was initially developed to help institutionalize the entrepreneurial activity as a systematic management process. Strategy was primarily seen as a problem to be defined and solved with Spock-like logic and precision, using the principles of rational planning. The major concepts of the time, like the BCG growth-share matrix or Porter's five-force framework, were all seen as new decision tools and technologies developed to help towards this end. Strategy was largely seen as a problem of market and product positioning. The sharpest analysts, with the most penetrating understanding of the underlying economic rules of the game, seemed best set to achieve and sustain superior corporate performance. Overall, management by the numbers was the main game. Harold Geneen and ITT were among its supreme players. It was a time when the Mr Spock side of the discipline's nature was firmly in charge, in both theory and practice, and the Vulcanization of the field seemed almost complete.

The Kirk era – the late 1980s and early 1990s

During the 1970s the seeds of a more humanist-interpretative view of strategy were already being sown in the work of Mintzberg, Quinn, Pettigrew and others. This emergent 'process' tradition challenged the rational-instrumental view about how strategy is actually developed in organizational settings. The implicit image of an all-powerful chief executive or top management team sitting in an office formulating strategy in strict logical sequence, setting objectives, identifying alternatives, selecting the optimum course of action, and then issuing directives for implementation, did not seem to fit with reality. This traditional 'command and control' image was also being challenged in practice. As the late Soichiro Honda once so colourfully put it:

> There is a limit to what can be thought out by big shots sitting at their desks. Where 100 people think there are 100 powers; if a 1000 people think there are 1000 powers.
>
> (Honda, cited in Alston 1989: 34)

For Quinn, Mintzberg and other process theorists, the development of strategy was seen as the product of many people, often with divergent views and interests, and the outcome was rarely independent of the people and the processes that produced it.

Strategic management, in their view, was more of a craft process than a planning one, with the notions of intuition, imagination, tacit knowledge and personal feel for the issues inherently important.

In the 1980s, as our thematic analysis of the key processes has consistently shown, this more humanist-interpretative view of strategy, the Captain Kirk side of the discipline's nature, came increasingly into prominence. Rational planning, in spite of its intellectual appeal, was not working as well as had been expected, and was shown to have very harmful side-effects when allowed to run amok. The overall picture was summed up by Anita Roddick of The Body Shop, as one of 'huge corporations' dying of 'boredom caused by the inertia of giantism', full of 'tired executives in tired systems' obsessed with 'corporate raiding, acquisitions of acres, strategies, niche markets, specialization and empire-building, where their only sense of adventure is in their profit and loss sheets' (Campbell 1994: 664). The tendency of the bureaucratic organization to substitute means for ends had become very pronounced in the case of many formal strategic planning systems. The search for comprehensive rationality seemed to demand loads of data, lots of form-filling, and risked paralysis by analysis. In short, for many companies the planning system had become the passion killer of the business.

Competitiveness in the 1980s was increasingly seen to be based on important aspects of the strategy process that lay well beyond the nostrums of the rational-planning era. The rational bureaucracy was recognized as presenting a difficult environment for innovation (Chapter 2). Innovation in large corporations, where it was happening at all, was most often to be found outside the formal planning system, in 'skunk works' or garage-type pockets of the organization, resourced by maverick fanatics, fired up mainly by the emotional excitement of the chase. The process of knowledge-generation itself was being seen in increasingly more humanistic terms, as the metaphorical or poetic approach of the Honda City design team illustrated (Chapter 3). During the 1980s, it was also becoming increasingly clear that the sustained competitive advantage enjoyed by many companies seemed to be based less on unique strategies or astute strategic positioning than on the management of key relationships. The enduring loyalty that Marks & Spencer, for example, enjoyed with customers, suppliers and employees was seen to be deeply rooted in the distinct corporate culture or value system of the company. The most inimitable aspects of this source of enduring competitive advantage were felt by many to be the least amenable to analysis and management in purely instrumental fashion (Chapter 5). From the specific examples of companies like Marks & Spencer and, more generally, from the increasing economic impact of the Japanese just-in-time philosophy, the strategy field rediscovered the potency of a more socialized view of inter-firm relationships. This ran counter to the purely rationalist perspective on the structure–competitiveness link, which characterized transaction-cost economics and related concepts. The strategic and economic benefits of trust were also to be found within organizations, in reduced overhead and more involved staff. Furthermore, new relationship-based strategies were also being seen to allow companies to enjoy market scale without bureaucratic mass, through the increasing use of strategic outsourcing and alliances (Chapter 4).

The late 1980s were also characterized by a renewed interest in leadership, the strategic significance of which had largely been lost during the Spock era, when techniques were prominent and the 'managerial mystique' prevailed. The success of companies like Wal-Mart, Turner Broadcasting and Microsoft, in outperforming well-entrenched incumbents, challenged the rational-economic perspective, and focused new attention on leadership and vision in competitive analysis (Chapter 5). Truly compelling vision was found to involve deep emotional resonance, stretching not only the muscles of the mind but also the sinews of the spirit. The strategy field discovered the competitive potency of more aesthetic values, the kind of values that make work really meaningful for most people. It also rediscovered the potency of pride and ambition, of Pepsi attacking Coke and Komatsu attacking Caterpillar, as much as anything because they were tired of being treated by the industry leaders as inferior 'imitators'. In contrast, many industry leaders, with clear economic advantages, were found to lack the compelling motivation (strategic intent) to be creative, and many frame-breaking innovations were seen to come from outside their ranks (Chapters 2, 5, and 6).

Coming to terms with the duality – a major challenge for the future

One of the enduring lessons from the more recent romantic and swash-buckling Kirk era is that attempts to over-rationalize and over-intellectualize strategy have been disappointing at best and harmful at worst. Furthermore, though most of the major concepts developed within the rational-economic perspective remain useful, few of the prescriptions based on these concepts have fully stood the test of time. The historical swing of the conceptual pendulum has, as we have seen, reflected the basic dialectical way in which knowledge has been created in the strategy field. It has also reflected the changing shape of the strategy problem over time. In the early decades, when industry structures were relatively stable, and barriers to entry and mobility relatively substantial, the essence of strategy tended to be about the selection of markets and market positions. Now with industry structures much more volatile, the strategy problem is being seen to be more about the selection and nurturing of core skills and processes, and the invention of markets to exploit these skills fully. The earlier notion of strategy as the technological silver bullet, or the megawatt marketing idea, has been giving way to a resource-based concept of competitive advantage, based upon the leveraging of the collective and cumulative power of people, processes and organizational learning (Chapter 3). What has perhaps been the most dramatic development in recent times has been the increasing experimentation with the federalist philosophy and form of organization, in efforts to find the best way to combine global scale with local diversity, and corporate integration with individual initiative (Chapter 4).

Why did it take the strategy field so long to import such potentially useful ideas from the realms of history and political philosophy? Perhaps it was because we have only recently really begun to appreciate the potential in the more artistic, humanist side of strategic management. However, our analysis also suggests that while the rational-economic view of strategy alone is clearly limited and self-defeating, so too is the more romantic and artistic view. Kirk in the ascendant may be just as dangerous, if not more so, than Spock. For example, value-rich charismatic leadership and corporate culture are very potent forces, but they have their own dangers, dark sides and potential excesses (Chapter 5). They can eventually become serious impediments to renewal, when the situation calls for it (Chapter 6). The recent experiences of companies like Digital and IBM, for example, are salutary lessons in the ultimate vulnerability of even value-rich leadership and corporate culture. The underlying economic rules of the game must be continually monitored and understood with Spock-like detachment, and no organization, however capable and confident, should delude itself into believing that it is ever in total control of its own destiny (Chapter 6). Nor should the Kirk side of strategy delude us into seeing strong leadership and culture as intrinsically virtuous (Chapter 5). The enlightenment of rationalism remains an important bulwark against the potential excesses of charisma and tradition. Charismatic leaders, as we have seen, are often troubled, obsessive spirits, and fear remains a powerful motivator in organizational life. Furthermore, while some organizations during the Kirk era were inspired to high performance by an elevating search for excellence, others were equally energized by a more basic passion for revenge. Honda's blood-curdling mission ('we will crush, squash, slaughter Yamaha' – Stalk 1988: 44) in the motorcycle wars of the early 1980s remains one of the most effective examples of compelling, gut-grabbing, vision in the history of the strategy field to date.

CONCLUSION

At the outset, we outlined why an examination of strategy and competitiveness based on the thematic analysis of five key processes was particularly appropriate in the current context. The field itself has been changing in focus over time, partly as a result of the accumulation of knowledge and partly because of the changing nature of its central concerns. Strategy remains a complex area. No single conceptual lens is likely to reveal all its important dimensions, and we have used many such lenses, in the form of themes and theories, throughout our process-by-process analysis. What this final reprise of the overall treatment has served to highlight is not only the strong cross-currents among the key processes underlying strategy, but also the duality that lies at the very core of the discipline: its rationalist and romantic nature.

The field now needs to come to terms with this duality, and move beyond the either-or debate that has characterized its development to date. We must now learn to view strategic management as a humanity as well as a science. We will have to see it encompassing the spiritual and emotional, as well as the intellectual and technological. In terms of our metaphor, Spock and Kirk are both needed on the bridge of the modern star-ship Enterprise, and we must find a way to work, both theoretically and practically, within this complex duality. The central concerns of strategic management continue to change over time, but its essence remains the generation of a sense of confidence, stability and direction in the face of uncertainty and change. We must be able to do this with all the rational-economic knowledge and strategic management technology that we can muster, but we must also do it with a clear sense of purpose. Increasingly in today's organizations we want to know not only where we are going but also why we are going there. We want to know what our organizations and our leaders stand for, as well as what they are trying to achieve, their values as well as visions, their beliefs as well as aspirations. In sum, what seems clear, from this final reprise, is that we now need strategists with not only analytical sharpness but also a well-developed sense of history and the human spirit. How to produce them will continue to challenge us all, educators, researchers and practitioners alike, for many years to come.

References

Abernathy, W.J. and Clark, K.B. (1985) 'Innovation: mapping the winds of creative destruction', *Research Policy* 14: 3–22.

Aldrich, H.E. (1979) *Organizations and Environments*, Englewood Cliffs, NJ: Prentice-Hall.

Allison, G.T. (1971) *Essence of Decision*, Boston: Little, Brown.

Alston, J. (1989) *The American Samurai*, New York: De Gruyter.

Anderson, P. and Tushman, M.L. (1990) 'Technological discontinuities and dominant designs: a cyclical model of technological change', *Administrative Science Quarterly* 35: 604–33.

Andrews, K.R. (1971) *The Concept of Corporate Strategy*, Homewood, Ill.: Irwin.

Ansoff, H.I. (1965) *Corporate Strategy*, New York: McGraw-Hill.

Ansoff, H.I. (1979) 'The changing shape of the strategy problem', *Journal of General Management* 4(4): 42–58.

Ansoff, H.I. (1987) *Corporate Strategy*, revised edn, Harmondsworth: Penguin.

Ansoff, H.I. (1991) 'Critique of Henry Mintzberg's "The design school: reconsidering the basic premises of strategic management"', *Strategic Management Journal* 12: 449–61.

Ansoff, H.I. (1994) 'Comment on Henry Mintzberg's "Rethinking strategic planning"', *Long Range Planning* 27(3): 31–2.

Antonioni, D. (1994) 'A new model of organizational change', *Organization Development Journal* 12(3): 17–28.

Appleyard, B. (1994) 'Deus ex machina', *Sunday Times Magazine*, 23 October: 21–30.

Argenti, J. (1980) *Practical Corporate Planning*, London: George Allen & Unwin.

Argyris, C. (1991) 'Teaching smart people how to learn', *Harvard Business Review* 69 (May–June): 99–109.

Argyris, C. and Schon, D.A. (1978) *Organizational Learning: A Theory of Action Perspective*, Reading, Mass.: Addison-Wesley.

Auletta, K. (1991) 'Schlumberger, Ltd.: Jean Riboud – excerpts from "A certain poetry"', in J.L. Bower, C.A. Bartlett, C.R. Christensen, A.E.

Pearson and K.R. Andrews, *Business Policy: Text and Cases*, 7th edn, Homewood, Ill.: Irwin.

Bahrami, H. (1992) 'The emerging flexible organization: perspectives from Silicon Valley', *California Management Review*, Summer: 33–52.

Barney, J.B. (1986) 'Organizational culture: can it be a source of sustained competitive advantage?', *Academy of Management Review* 11(3): 656–65.

Barney, J.B. (1991) 'Firm resources and sustained competitive advantage', *Journal of Management* 17(1): 99–120.

Barney, J.B. and Ouchi, W.G. (1986) *Organizational Economics*, San Francisco: Jossey-Bass.

Barr, P.S., Stimpert, J.L. and Huff, A.S. (1992) 'Cognitive change, strategic action, and organizational renewal', *Strategic Management Journal* 13S: 15–36.

Bartlett, C.A. and Ghoshal, S. (1990) 'Matrix management: not a structure, a frame of mind', *Harvard Business Review* 68 (July–August): 138–45.

Bartlett, C.A. and Ghoshal, S. (1993) 'Beyond the M-form: toward a managerial theory of the firm', *Strategic Management Journal* 14: 23–46.

Bartlett, C.A. and Ghoshal, S. (1994) 'Changing the role of top management: beyond strategy to purpose', *Harvard Business Review* 72 (November–December): 79–88.

Bean, T.J. and Gros, J.G. (1992) 'R&D benchmarking at AT&T', *Research/Technology Management* 35(4): 32–7.

Beck, N. (1992) *Shifting Gears: Thriving in the New Economy*, Toronto: HarperCollins.

Beckhard, R. and Harris, R.T. (1987) *Organizational Transitions*, 2nd edn, Reading, Mass.: Addison-Wesley.

Bennis, W. and Nanus, B. (1985) *Leaders: The Strategies for Taking Charge*, New York: Harper & Row.

Bettis, R.A. and Hall, W.K. (1983) 'The business portfolio approach – where it falls down in practice', *Long Range Planning* 16(2): 95–104.

Biggart, N.W. and Hamilton, G.G. (1987) 'An institutional theory of leadership', *Journal of Applied Behavioural Science* 23(4): 429–41.

Boeker, W. (1989) 'Strategic change: the effects of founding and history', *Academy of Management Journal* 32(3): 489–515.

Bolton, M.K. (1993a) 'Imitation versus innovation: lessons to be learned from the Japanese', *Organizational Dynamics* 22 (Winter): 30–45.

Bolton, M.K. (1993b) 'Organizational innovation and substandard performance: when is necessity the mother of innovation?', *Organization Science* 4(1): 57–75.

Bower, J.L. (1970) *Managing the Resource Allocation Process*, Homewood, Ill.: Irwin.

Bower, J.L. and Christensen, C.M. (1995) 'Disruptive technologies: catching the wave', *Harvard Business Review* 73 (January–February): 43–53.

Bower, J.L. and Harris, C. (1991) 'Marks and Spencer, Ltd.', in J.L. Bower, C.A. Bartlett, C.R. Christensen, A.E. Pearson, and K.R. Andrews, *Business Policy: Text and Cases*, 7th edn, Homewood, Ill.: Irwin.

Brown, J.S. (1991) 'Research that reinvents the corporation', *Harvard Business Review* 69 (January–February): 102–11.

Brunsson, N. (1982) 'The irrationality of action and action rationality: decisions, ideologies and organizational action', *Journal of Management Studies* 19(1): 29–44.

Bryman, A. (1993) 'Charismatic leadership in business organizations: some neglected issues', *Leadership Quarterly* 4(3/4): 289–304.

Burch, J. (1986) 'Profiling the entrepreneur', *Business Horizons*, September–October: 13–16.

Burgleman, R.A. (1983a) 'A process model of internal corporate venturing in the diversified major firm', *Administrative Science Quarterly* 28: 223–44.

Burgleman, R.A. (1983b) 'A model of the interaction of strategic behaviour, corporate context and the concept of strategy', *Academy of Management Review* 8(1): 61–70.

Burns, J.M. (1978) *Leadership*, New York: Harper & Row.

Burns, T. and Stalker, G.M. (1966) *The Management of Innovation*, London: Tavistock.

Butcher, L. (1988) *Accidental Millionaire*, New York: Paragon House Publications.

Buzzell, R. and Gale, B. (1987) *The PIMS Principles*, New York: Free Press.

Calori, R. and Sarnin, P. (1991) 'Corporate culture and economic performance', *Organization Studies* 12(1): 49–74.

Campbell, A. (1994) 'The Body Shop International – the most honest cosmetic company in the world', case reproduced in B. De Wit and R. Meyer, *Strategy*, Minneapolis/St Paul, Minn.: West Publishing Company.

Campbell, A., Goold, M. and Alexander, M. (1995) 'Corporate strategy: the quest for parenting advantage', *Harvard Business Review* 73 (March–April): 120–32.

Carroll, G.R. (1994) 'Organizations ... the smaller they get', *California Management Review* 37(1): 28–41.

Chakravarthy, B.S. (1982) 'Adaptation: a promising metaphor for strategic management', *Academy of Management Review* 7(1): 35–44.

Chandler, A.D. (1962) *Strategy and Structure: Chapters in the History of the American Industrial Enterprise*, Cambridge, Mass.: MIT Press.

Chandler, A.D. (1977) *The Visible Hand: The Managerial Revolution in American Business*, Cambridge, Mass.: Harvard University Press.

Chandler, A.D. (1990) 'The enduring logic of industrial success', *Harvard Business Review* 68 (March–April): 130–40.

Chandler, A.D. (1991) 'The functions of the HQ unit in the multi-business firm', *Strategic Management Journal* 12: 31–50.

Channon, D. (1973) *Strategy and Structure in British Enterprise*, Boston: Graduate School of Business Administration, Harvard University.

Chew, W.B., Leonard-Barton, D. and Bohn, R.E. (1991) 'Beating Murphy's Law', *Sloan Management Review*, Spring: 5–16.

Child, J. and Smith, C. (1987) 'The context and process of organizational transformation – Cadbury Limited in its sector', *Journal of Management Studies* 24(6): 565–93.

Clegg, S.R. (1990) *Modern Organizations: Organization Studies in the Postmodern World*, London: Sage.

Cohen, W.M. and Levinthal, D.A. (1990) 'Absorptive capacity: a new perspective on learning and innovation', *Administrative Science Quarterly* 35: 128–52.

Collins, J.C. and Porras, J.I. (1991) 'Organizational vision and visionary organizations', *California Management Review*, Fall: 30–52.

Conger, J.A. and Kanungo, R.N. (1987) 'Toward a behavioral theory of charismatic leadership in organizational settings', *Academy of Management Review* 12(4): 637–47.

Conner, K.R. (1991) 'A historical comparison of resource-based theory and five schools of thought within industrial organization economics: do we have a new theory of the firm?', *Journal of Management* 17(1): 121–54.

Cyert, R.M. and March, J.G. (1963) *A Behavioral Theory of the Firm*, Englewood Cliffs, NJ: Prentice-Hall.

Czarniawska-Joerges, B. and Wolf, R. (1991) 'Leaders, managers, and entrepreneurs on and off the organizational stage', *Organizational Studies* 12(4): 529–46.

Dalton, D.R. and Kesner, I.F. (1985) 'Organizational performance as an antecedent of inside/outside chief executive succession: an empirical assessment', *Academy of Management Journal* 28(4): 749–62.

Davis, S.M. and Lawrence, P.R. (1978) 'Problems of matrix organizations', *Harvard Business Review* 56 (May–June): 131–42.

Day, G.S. (1994) 'Continuous learning about markets', *California Management Review*, Summer: 9–31.

Deal, T.E. and Kennedy, A.A. (1982) *Corporate Cultures*, Reading, Mass.: Addison-Wesley.

DeBresson, C. and Amesse, F. (1991) 'Networks of innovators: a review and introduction to the issue', *Research Policy* 20: 363–79.

de Geus, A.P. (1988) 'Planning as learning', *Harvard Business Review* 66 (March–April): 70–4.

Denison, D.R. (1984) 'Bringing corporate culture to the bottom line', *Organizational Dynamics*, Autumn: 5–22.

de Pree, M. (1989) *Leadership is an Art*, New York: Doubleday.

Dodgson, M. (1993) 'Organizational learning: a review of some literature', *Organization Studies* 14(3): 375–94.

Donaldson, L. (1990) 'The ethereal hand: organizational economics and management theory', *Academy of Management Review* 15(3): 369–81.

Doz, Y.L. and Prahalad, C.K. (1991) 'Managing DMNCs: a search for a new paradigm', *Strategic Management Journal* 12: 145–64.

Drucker, P.F. (1985) *Innovation and Entrepreneurship*, London: William Heinemann.

Drucker, P.F. (1991) 'The new productivity challenge', *Harvard Business Review* 69 (November–December): 69–79.

Dumaine, B. (1993) 'America's toughest bosses', *Fortune*, 18 October: 44–51.

Dunphy, D.C. and Stace, D.A. (1988) 'Transformational and coercive strategies for planned organizational change: beyond the OD model', *Organization Studies* 9(3): 317–34.

Dyer, J.H. and Ouchi, W.G. (1993) 'Japanese-style partnerships: giving companies a competitive edge', *Sloan Management Review*, Fall: 51–63.

Ebers, M. (1985) 'Understanding organizations: the poetic mode', *Journal of Management* 11(2): 51–62.

Eitzen, D.S. and Yetman, N.R. (1972) 'Managerial change, longevity and organizational effectiveness', *Administrative Science Quarterly* 17: 110–16.

Evan, W.M. and Olk, P. (1990) 'R&D consortia: a new US organizational form', *Sloan Management Review*, Spring: 37–46.

Fiedler, F.E. (1965) 'Engineer the job to fit the manager', *Harvard Business Review* 43 (September–October): 115–22.

Fiedler, F.E. (1967) *A Theory of Leadership Effectiveness*, New York: McGraw-Hill.

Fiol, C.M. and Lyles, M.A. (1985) 'Organizational learning', *Academy of Management Review* 10(4): 803–13.

Fitzgerald, T.H. (1988) 'Can change in organizational culture really be managed?', *Organizational Dynamics* 17(2): 5–15.

Foster, R.N. (1986) *Innovation: The Attacker's Advantage*, New York: Summit Books.

Gagliardi, P. (1986) 'The creation and change of organizational cultures: a conceptual framework', *Organization Studies* 7(2): 117–34.

Galbraith, J.K. (1956) *American Capitalism: The Concept of Countervailing Power* (2nd edn), Boston: Houghton Mifflin.

Galbraith, J.R. (1971) 'Matrix organizational designs', *Business Horizons* 15(1): 29–40.

Garvin, D.A. (1993) 'Building a learning organization', *Harvard Business Review* 71 (July–August): 78–91.

Gemmill, G. and Oakley, J. (1992) 'Leadership: an alienating social myth', *Human Relations* 45(2): 113–29.

Gersick, C.J.G. (1991) 'Revolutionary change theories: a multilevel exploration of the punctuated equilibrium paradigm', *Academy of Management Review* 16(1): 10–36.

Ghemawat, P. (1985) 'Building strategy on the experience curve', *Harvard Business Review* 63 (March–April): 143–9.

Ghoshal, S. (1989) *Scandinavian Airline System (SAS) in 1988*, Case No. 389-025-1N, INSEAD.

Ghoshal, S. and Mintzberg, H. (1994) 'Diversifiction and diversifact', *California Management Review* 37(1), Fall: 8–27.

Ginsberg, A. and Abrahamson, E. (1991) 'Champions of change and strategic shifts: the role of internal and external advocates', *Journal of Management Studies* 28(2): 173–90.

Gomes-Casseres, B. (1994) 'Group versus group: how alliance networks compete', *Harvard Business Review* 72 (July–August): 62–74.

Goodstein, L.D. and Burke, W.W. (1991) 'Creating successful organizational change', *Organizational Dynamics* 19(4): 5–17.

Goold, M. (1991) 'Strategic control in the decentralized firm', *Sloan Management Review*, Winter: 69–81.

Goold, M. and Campbell, A. (1987) *Strategies and Styles: the Role of the Center in Diversified Companies*, Oxford: Basil Blackwell.

Gordon, G.G. (1991) 'Industry determinants of organizational culture', *Academy of Management Review* 16(2): 396–415.

Granovetter, M. (1985) 'Economic action and social structure: the problem of embeddedness', *American Journal of Sociology* 91(3): 481–510.

Grant, R.M. (1991) 'The resource-based theory of competitive advantage:

implications for strategy formulation', *California Management Review*, Spring: 114–35.

Gras, N.S.B. (1949) 'Leadership, past and present', *Harvard Business Review* 27(4): 419–37.

Greenwood, R. and Hinings, C.R. (1988) 'Organizational design types, tracks and the dynamics of change', *Organization Studies* 9(3): 293–316.

Greiner, L.E. (1972) 'Evolution and revolution as organizations grow', *Harvard Business Review* 50 (July–August): 37–46.

Grinyer, P. and McKiernan, P. (1990) 'Generating major change in stagnating companies', *Strategic Management Journal* 11: 131–46.

Grinyer, P.H. and Spender, J.C. (1979) 'Recipes, crises, and adaptation in mature businesses', *International Studies of Management and Organization* IX(3): 113–33.

Hall, W.K. (1978) 'SBUs: hot new topic in the management of diversification', *Business Horizons* 21(1): 17–25.

Hambrick, D.C. (ed.) (1989) 'Strategic leadership', *Strategic Management Journal* (Special Issue) 10S: 1–172.

Hambrick, D.C. and Fukutomi, G.D.S. (1991) 'The seasons of a CEO's tenure', *Academy of Management Review* 16(4): 719–42.

Hamel, G. (1991) 'Competition for competence and inter-partner learning within international strategic alliances', *Strategic Management Journal* 12: 83–103.

Hamel, G. and Prahalad, C.K. (1989) 'Strategic intent', *Harvard Business Review* 67 (May–June): 63–76.

Hamel, G., Doz, Y.L. and Prahalad, C.K. (1989) 'Collaborate with your competitors – and win', *Harvard Business Review* 67 (January–February): 133–9.

Hamermesh, R.G. and Christiansen, E.T. (1976) PC&D Inc., Case No. 9-038-072, Harvard Business School.

Hamermesh, R.G., Gordon, K. and Reed, J.P. (1978) Crown Cork and Seal Co. Inc., Case No. 9-378-024, Harvard Business School.

Hammer, M. (1990) 'Reengineering work: don't automate, obliterate', *Harvard Business Review* 68 (July–August): 104–12.

Hammer, M. and Champy, J. (1993) *Reengineering the Corporation*, New York: Harper Business.

Handy, C. (1992) 'Balancing corporate power: a new federalist paper', *Harvard Business Review* 70 (November–December): 59–72.

Hannan, M.T. and Freeman, J. (1977) 'The population ecology of organizations', *American Journal of Sociology* 82(5): 929–64.

Hannan, M.T. and Freeman, J. (1984) 'Structural inertia and organizational change', *American Sociological Review* 49: 149–64.

Hawkins, P. (1994) 'Organizational learning: taking stock and facing the challenge', *Management Learning* 25(1): 71–82.

Hedberg, B. (1981) 'How organizations learn and unlearn', in P.C. Nystrom and W.H. Starbuck (eds) *Handbook of Organizational Design*, Vol. 1, New York: Oxford University Press.

Henderson, B. (1973) 'The experience curve revisited: the growth share matrix of the product portfolio', *Perspectives*, Boston Consulting Group.

Hill, C.W.L. (1990) 'Cooperation, opportunism, and the invisible hand:

implications for transaction cost theory', *Academy of Management Review* 15(3): 500–13.

Hirschhorn, L. and Gilmore, T. (1992) 'The new boundaries of the boundaryless company', *Harvard Business Review* 70 (May–June): 104–15.

Hofer, C.W. (1977) 'Conceptual constructs for formulating corporate and business strategies', Case No. 9-378-354, Boston: Intercollegiate Case Clearing House.

Hoffman, R.C. (1989) 'Strategies for corporate turnarounds: what do we know about them?', *Journal of General Management* 14(3): 46–66.

Hopfl, H. (1992) 'The making of the corporate acolyte: some thoughts on charismatic leadership and the reality of organizational commitment', *Journal of Management Studies* 29(1): 23–33.

Horsley, W. and Buckley, R. (1990) *Nippon New Superpower: Japan Since 1945*, London: BBC Books.

House, R.J., Spangler, W.D. and Woycke, J. (1991) 'Personality and charisma in the US presidency: a psychological theory of leadership effectiveness', *Administrative Science Quarterly* 36: 364–96.

Howard, R. (1992) 'The CEO as organizational architect: an interview with Xerox's Paul Allaire', *Harvard Business Review* 70 (September–October): 107–21.

Huber, G.P. (1991) 'Organizational learning: the contributing processes and the literatures', *Organization Science* 2(1): 88–115.

Jacobson, R. (1992) 'The Austrian school of strategy', *Academy of Management Review* 17(4): 782–807.

Jago, A.G. (1982) 'Leadership: perspectives in theory and research', *Management Science* 28(3): 315–36.

Jarillo, J.C. (1988) 'On strategic networks', *Strategic Management Journal* 9: 31–41.

Johnson, G. (1988) 'Rethinking incrementalism', *Strategic Management Journal* 9: 75–91.

Johnson, G. (1990) 'Managing strategic change: the role of symbolic action', *British Journal of Management* 1: 183–200.

Jorde, T.M. and Teece, D.J. (1989) 'Competition and cooperation: striking the right balance', *California Management Review,* Spring: 25–37.

Kanter, R.M. (1982) 'The middle manager as innovator', *Harvard Business Review* 60 (July–August): 95–105.

Kanter, R.M. (1983) *The Change Masters*, New York: Simon & Schuster.

Kanter, R.M. (1988) 'When a thousand flowers bloom: structural, collective and social conditions for innovation in organizations', *Research in Organization Behavior* 10: 169–211.

Kanter, R.M. (1991) 'Change: where to begin', *Harvard Business Review* 69 (July–August): 8–9.

Kaplan, R. (1987) 'Entrepreneurship reconsidered: the antimanagement bias', *Harvard Business Review* 65 (May–June): 84–9.

Katz, D. and Kahn, R.L. (1978) *The Social Psychology of Organizations*, 2nd edn, New York: John Wiley.

Kennedy, C. (1989) 'The transformation of AT&T', *Long Range Planning* 22(3): 10–17.

Kets de Vries, M.F.R. (1990) 'The organizational fool: balancing a leader's hubris', *Human Relations* 43(8): 751–70.

Kets de Vries, M.F.R. and Miller, D. (1985) 'Narcissism and leadership: an object relations perspective', *Human Relations* 38(6): 583–601.

Kidder, T. (1981) *The Soul of a New Machine*, Boston: Little, Brown & Co.

Kim, D.H. (1993) 'The link between individual and organizational learning', *Sloan Management Review*, Fall: 37–50.

Kimberly, J.R. (1979) 'Issues in the creation of organizations: initiation, innovation and institutionalization', *Academy of Management Journal* 22(3): 437–57.

Kofman, F. and Senge, P.M. (1993) 'Communities of commitment: the heart of learning organizations', *Organizational Dynamics* 22, Autumn: 5–23.

Kotter, J.P. (1982) *The General Managers*, New York: Free Press.

Kotter, J.P. (1990) 'What leaders really do', *Harvard Business Review* 68 (May–June): 103–11.

Kuhnert, K.W. and Lewis, P. (1987) 'Transactional and transformative leadership: a constructive/developmental analysis', *Academy of Management Review* 12(4): 648–57.

Leavy, B. (1991a) 'The three Cs of competitive retailing', in H.E. Glass and M.A. Hovde (eds) *Handbook of Business Strategy* (1991/92 Yearbook), Boston: Warren Gorham & Lamont.

Leavy, B. (1991b) 'A process study of strategic change and industry evolution – the case of the Irish Dairy Industry 1958–74', *British Journal of Management* 2(4): 187–204.

Leavy, B. (1992) 'Strategic vision and inspirational leadership', in H.E. Glass and M.A. Hovde (eds) *Handbook of Business Strategy* (1992/93 Yearbook), Boston: Warren Gorham & Lamont.

Leavy, B. (1994) 'Two strategic perspectives on the buyer–supplier relationship', *Production and Inventory Management Journal* 35(2): 47–51.

Leavy, B. (1995a) 'Symbol and substance in strategic leadership', *Journal of General Management* 20(4): 40–53.

Leavy, B (1995b) 'Strategy, but not as we know it', *World Link*, July–August: 30–5

Leavy, B. and Wilson, D. (1994) *Strategy and Leadership*, London: Routledge.

Lei, D. and Slocum, J.W. (1992) 'Global strategy, competence-building and strategic alliances', *California Management Review*, Fall: 81–97.

Leonard-Barton, D. (1992a) 'The factory as a learning laboratory', *Sloan Management Review*, Fall: 23–38.

Leonard-Barton, D. (1992b) 'Core capabilities and core rigidities: a paradox in managing new product development', *Strategic Management Journal* 13: 111–25.

Levitt, B. and March, J.G. (1988) 'Organizational learning', *Annual Review of Sociology* 14: 319–40.

Lewin, K. (1951) *Field Theory in Social Science*, New York: Harper & Row.

Lieberson, S. and O'Connor, J.F. (1972) 'Leadership and organizational performance: a study of large corporations', *American Sociological Review* 37: 117–30.

Louis, M.R. (1981) 'A cultural perspective on organizations: the need for and consequences of viewing organizations as culture-bearing milieux', *Human Systems Management* 2: 246–58.

Lukes, S. (1974) *Power: A Radical View*, London: Macmillan.

McKee, D. (1992) 'An organizational learning approach to product innovation', *Journal of Product Innovation Management* 9: 232–45.

Mahoney, J.T. and Pandian, J.R. (1992) 'The resource-based view within the conversation of strategic management', *Strategic Management Journal* 13: 363–80.

Maidique, M.A. (1980) 'Entrepreneurs, champions, and technological innovation', *Sloan Management Review*, Winter: 59–76.

March, J.G. (1962) 'The business firm as a political coalition', *The Journal of Politics* 24: 662–78.

March, J.G. (1981) 'Footnotes to organizational change', *Administrative Science Quarterly* 26: 563–77.

March, J.G. and Simon, H.A. (1958) *Organizations*, New York: John Wiley.

Meindl, J.R., Ehrlich, S.B. and Dukerich, J.M. (1985) 'The romance of leadership', *Administrative Science Quarterly* 30: 78–102.

Meyer, A.D. (1982) 'How ideologies supplant formal structures and shape responses to environments', *Journal of Management Studies* 19(1): 45–61.

Meyer, A.D. (1991) 'What is strategy's distinctive competence?', *Journal of Management* 17(4): 821–33.

Meyer, A.D., Brooks, G.R. and Goes, J.B. (1990) 'Environmental jolts and industry revolution: organizational responses to discontinuous change', *Strategic Management Journal* 11: 93–110.

Meyer, J.W. and Rowan, B. (1977) 'Institutionalized organizations: formal structure as myth and ceremony', *American Journal of Sociology* 83(2): 340–63.

Miles, R.E. and Snow, C.C. (1978) *Organizational Strategy, Structure and Process*, New York: McGraw-Hill.

Miles, R.E. and Snow, C.C. (1992) 'Causes of failure in network organizations', *California Management Review*, Summer: 53–72.

Miller, D. (1982) 'Evolution and revolution : a quantum view of structural change in organizations', *Journal of Management Studies* 19(2): 131–51.

Miller, D. (1986) 'Configurations of strategy and structure: towards a synthesis', *Strategic Management Journal* 7: 233–49.

Miller, D. (1990) *The Icarus Paradox*, New York: Harper Business.

Miller, D. (1991) 'Stale in the saddle: CEO tenure and the match between organization and environment', *Management Science* 37(1): 34–52.

Miller, D. and Friesen, P.H. (1980) 'Momentum and revolution in organizational adaptation', *Academy of Management Journal* 23(4): 591–614.

Mintzberg, H. (1978) 'Patterns in strategy formation', *Management Science* 24(9): 934–48.

Mintzberg, H. (1981) 'Organization design: fashion or fit?', *Harvard Business Review* 59 (January–February): 103–16.

Mintzberg, H. (1987) 'Crafting strategy', *Harvard Business Review* 65 (July–August): 66–75.

Mintzberg, H. (1990) 'The design school: reconsidering the basic premises of strategic management', *Strategic Management Journal* 11: 171–95.

Mintzberg, H. (1991a) 'The effective organization: forces and forms', *Sloan Management Review*, Winter: 54–67.

Mintzberg, H. (1991b) 'Learning 1, planning 0: reply to Igor Ansoff', *Strategic Management Journal* 12: 463–66.

Mintzberg, H. (1994a) *The Rise and Fall of Strategic Planning*, Englewood Cliffs, NJ: Prentice-Hall.

Mintzberg, H. (1994b) 'Rethinking strategic planning', *Long Range Planning* 27(3): 12–30.

Mito, S. (1990) *The Honda Book of Management*, London: The Athlone Press.

Mitsch, R.A. (1992) 'R&D at 3M: continuing to play a big role', *Research/Technology Management* 35(5): 22–6.

Morita, A. (1986) *Made In Japan*, Glasgow: William Collins.

Morris, M.H. and Trotter, J.D. (1990) 'Institutionalizing entrepreneurship in a large company: a case study at AT&T', *Industrial Marketing Management* 19(3): 595–612.

Murphy, P.E. (1994) 'European managers' views on corporate ethics', *Business Ethics: A European Review* 3(3): 137–144.

Murray, E.A. (1978) 'Strategic choice as a negotiated outcome', *Management Science* 24(9): 960–72.

Nanus, B. (1992) *Visionary Leadership*, San Francisco: Jossey-Bass.

Narayanan, V.K. and Fahey, L. (1982) 'The micro-politics of strategy formulation', *Academy of Management Review* 7(1): 25–34.

Nathanson, D. and Cassano, J. (1982) 'Organization, diversity, and performance', *Wharton Magazine*, Summer: 19–26.

Nixon, R.M. (1982) *Leaders*, London: Sidgwick & Jackson.

Noel, A. (1989) 'Strategic cores and magnificent obsessions: discovering strategy formation through daily activities of CEOs', *Strategic Management Journal* 10S: 33–49.

Nonaka, I. (1988a) 'Creating organizational order out of chaos: self-renewal in Japanese firms', *California Management Review*, Spring: 57–73.

Nonaka, I. (1988b) 'Towards middle-up-down management: accelerating information creation', *Sloan Management Review*, Spring: 9–18.

Nonaka, I. (1991) 'The knowledge-creating company', *Harvard Business Review* 69 (November–December): 96–104.

Nonaka, I. (1994) 'A dynamic theory of organizational knowledge creation', *Organization Science* 5, 1: 14–37.

Norburn, D. (1989) 'The chief executive: a breed apart', *Strategic Management Journal* 10: 1–15.

Normann, R. and Ramirez, R. (1993) 'From value chain to value constellation: designing interactive strategy', *Harvard Business Review* 71 (July–August): 65–77.

Nystrom, P.C. and Starbuck, W.H. (1984) 'To avoid organizational crises, unlearn', *Organizational Dynamics* 12: 53–65.

Ohmae, K. (1989a) 'The global logic of strategic alliances', *Harvard Business Review* 67 (March–April): 143–54.

Ohmae, K. (1989b) 'Planting for a global harvest', *Harvard Business Review* 67 (July–August): 136–45.

Ohmae, K. (1990) *The Borderless World*, Harper Business.

O'Neill, H.M. (1986) 'Turnaround and recovery: what strategy do you need?', *Long Range Planning* 19(1): 80–6.

O'Reilly, C. (1989) 'Corporations, culture, and commitment: motivation and social control in organizations', *California Management Review*, Summer: 9–41.

Osborne, R.L. (1991) 'The dark side of the entrepreneur', *Long Range Planning* 24(3): 26–31.

Ostroff, F. and Smith, D. (1992) 'The horizontal organization', *The McKinsey Quarterly* 1: 148–68.

Owen, G. and Harrison, T. (1995) 'Why ICI chose to demerge', *Harvard Business Review* 73 (March–April): 133–42.

Painton, P. (1992) 'The taming of Ted Turner', *Time*, 6 January: 28–34.

Pascale, R.T. (1984) 'Perspectives on strategy: the real story behind Honda's success', *California Management Review* XXVI(3): 47–72.

Pascale, R.T. (1985) 'The paradox of corporate culture: reconciling ourselves to socialization', *California Management Review* 27(2), Winter: 26–41.

Pascale, R.T. and Athos, A.G. (1981) *The Art of Japanese Management*, New York: Simon & Schuster.

Pauchant, T.C. (1991) 'Transferential leadership: towards a more complex understanding of charisma in organizations', *Organization Studies* 12(4): 507–27.

Pearson, A.E. and Ehrlich, S.P. (1990) Honda Motor Company and Honda of America, Case No. 9-390-111, Harvard Business School.

Pearson, A.E., Boneysteele, P. and Nurme, D. (1990) *Pepsi-Cola U.S. Beverages (A)*, Case No. 9-390-034, Harvard Business School.

Penrose, E.T. (1959) *The Theory of the Growth of the Firm*, New York: John Wiley.

Peteraf, M.A. (1993) 'The cornerstones of competitive advantage: a resource-based view', *Strategic Management Journal* 14: 179–91.

Peters, T. (1984) 'Strategy follows structure: developing distinctive skills', *California Management Review* XXVI(3): 111–25.

Peters, T. (1990) 'Get innovative or get dead' (Part 1), *California Management Review* 33(1), Fall: 9–26.

Peters, T. (1991) 'Get innovative or get dead' (Part 2), *California Management Review* 33(2), Winter: 9–23.

Peters, T. (1992a) *Liberation Management*, London: Macmillan.

Peters, T. (1992b) 'Rethinking scale', *California Management Review*, Fall: 7–29.

Peters, T.J. and Waterman, R.H. (1982) *In Search Of Excellence*, New York: Harper & Row.

Pettigrew, A.M. (1977) 'Strategy formulation as a political process', *International Studies of Management and Organization* 7(2): 78–87.

Pettigrew, A.M. (1985) *The Awakening Giant*, Oxford: Basil Blackwell.

Pettigrew, A.M. (1987) 'Context and action in the transformation of the firm', *Journal of Management Studies* 24(6): 649–70.

Pfeffer, J. (1992) 'Understanding power in organizations', *California Management Review*, Winter: 29–50.

Pfeffer, J. and Salancik, G.R. (1978) *The External Control of Organizations*, New York: Harper & Row.

Pooley-Dias, G. (1972) 'The strategy and structure of French industrial enterprise', Doctoral dissertation, Harvard Business School.

Porter, M.E. (1980) *Competitive Strategy*, New York: Free Press.

Porter, M.E. (1981) 'The contributions of industrial organization to strategic management', *Academy of Management Review* 6: 609–20.

Porter, M.E. (1985) *Competitive Advantage*, New York: Free Press.

Porter, M.E. (1987) 'From competitive advantage to corporate strategy', *Harvard Business Review* 65 (May–June): 43–59.

Porter, M.E. (1990) *The Competitive Advantage of Nations*, London: Macmillan.

Porter, M.E. (1991) 'Towards a dynamic theory of strategy', *Strategic Management Journal* 12S: 95–117.

Powell, W.W. (1990) 'Neither market nor hierarchy', *Research in Organizational Behaviour* 12: 295–336.

Prahalad, C.K. and Bettis, R.A. (1986) 'The dominant logic: a new linkage between diversity and performance', *Strategic Management Journal* 7(6): 485–501.

Prahalad, C.K. and Hamel, G. (1990) 'The core competence of the corporation', *Harvard Business Review* 68: 79–91.

Prahalad, C.K. and Hamel, G. (1994) 'Strategy as a field of study: why search for a new paradigm?', *Strategic Management Journal* 15: 5–16.

Quinn, J.B. (1978) 'Strategic change: logical incrementalism', *Sloan Management Review*, Fall: 7–21.

Quinn, J.B. (1979) 'Technological innovation, entrepreneurship, and strategy', *Sloan Management Review*, Spring: 19–30.

Quinn, J.B. (1980) *Strategies for Change: Logical Incrementalism*, Homewood Ill.: Irwin.

Quinn, J.B. (1982) 'Managing strategies incrementally', *Omega* 10(6): 613–27.

Quinn, J.B. (1985) 'Managing innovation: controlled chaos', *Harvard Business Review*, May–June: 73–84.

Quinn, J.B. (1989) 'Strategic change: logical incrementalism' (reprint with retrospective commentary), *Sloan Management Review*, Summer: 45–60.

Quinn, J.B. and Hilmer, F.G. (1994) 'Strategic outsourcing', *Sloan Management Review*, Summer: 43–55.

Quinn, J.B. and Paquette, P.C. (1990) 'Technology in services: creating organizational revolutions', *Sloan Management Review*, Winter: 67–78.

Quinn, J.B., Doorley, T.L. and Paquette, P.C. (1990a) 'Technology in services: rethinking strategic focus', *Sloan Management Review*, Winter: 79–87.

Quinn, J.B., Doorley, T.L. and Paquette, P.C. (1990b) 'Beyond products: services-based strategy', *Harvard Business Review* 68 (March–April): 58–67.

Ray, C.A. (1986) 'Corporate culture: the last frontier of control', *Journal of Management Studies* 23(3): 287–98.

Rebello, K., Schwartz, E.I., Verity, J.W., Lewyn, M. and Levine, J. (1993) 'Is Microsoft too powerful?', *Business Week*, 1 March: 48–55.

Reich, R.B. (1987) 'Entrepreneurship reconsidered: the team as hero', *Harvard Business Review* 65 (May–June): 77–83.

Reich, R.B. and Mankin, E.D. (1986) 'Joint ventures with Japan give away our future', *Harvard Business Review* 64 (March–April): 78–86.

Robbins, D.K. and Pearce, J.A. (1992) 'Turnaround: retrenchment and recovery', *Strategic Management Journal* 13: 287–309.

Roberts, N.C. (1985) 'Transforming leadership: a process of collective action', *Human Relations* 38(11): 1023–46.

Robinson, S.J.Q., Hichens, R.E. and Wade, D.P. (1978) 'The directional policy matrix – tool for strategic planning', *Long Range Planning* 11(3): 8–15.

Rosenberg, N. and Steinmueller, W.E. (1988) 'Why Americans are such poor imitators', *American Economic Review* 78: 229–34.

Rumelt, R.P. (1974) *Strategy, Structure and Economic Performance*, Boston: Division of Research, Graduate School of Business Administration, Harvard University.

Rumelt, R.P., Schendel, D. and Teece, D.J. (1991) 'Strategic management and economics', *Strategic Management Journal* 12S: 5–29.

Saffold, G.S. (1988) 'Cultural traits, strength, and organizational performance: moving beyond strong culture', *Academy of Management Review* 13(4): 546–58.

Saxenian, A. (1991) 'The origins and dynamics of production networks in Silicon Valley', *Research Policy* 20: 423–37.

Schaffer, R.H. and Thompson, H.A. (1992) 'Successful change programs begin with results', *Harvard Business Review* 70 (January–February): 80–9.

Schendel, D.E. and Hofer, C.W. (1979) *Strategic Management: A New View of Business Policy and Planning*, Boston: Little, Brown & Co.

Schlesinger, L.A., Pelofsky, M., Pascale, R.T. and Ehrlich, S.P. (1990) The transformation at Ford, Case No. 9-390-083, Harvard Business School.

Schneiderman, H.A. (1991) 'Managing R&D: a perspective from the top', *Sloan Management Review*, Summer: 53–8.

Schoeffler, S., Buzell, R.D. and Heany, D.F. (1974) 'Impact of strategic planning on profit performance', *Harvard Business Review* 52 (March–April): 137–45.

Schroeder, D.M. and Robinson, A.G. (1991) 'America's most successful export to Japan: continuous improvement programs', *Sloan Management Review*, Spring: 67–81.

Schumpeter, J.A. (1934) *The Theory of Economic Development*, Oxford: Oxford University Press.

Sculley, J. (1987) *Odyssey: Pepsi to Apple* (with J.A. Byrne), London: Fontana.

Selznick, P. (1957) *Leadership in Administration*, Evanston, Ill.: Row, Peterson.

Senge, P.M. (1990a) 'The leader's new work: building learning organizations', *Sloan Management Review*, Fall: 7–23.

Senge, P.M. (1990b) *The Fifth Discipline: The Art and Practice of the Learning Organization*, New York: Doubleday.

Senge, P.M. (1993) 'Harnessing the power of organizational learning', *Network* 6(6): 4–5.

Sheldon, A. (1980) 'Organizational paradigms: a theory of organizational change', *Organizational Dynamics*, Winter: 61–80.

Sherman, S. (1993) 'A master class in radical change', *Fortune*, 13 December: 40–4.

Shetty, Y.K. and Perry, N.S. (1976) 'Are top executives transferable across companies?', *Business Horizons* 19(3), June: 23–8.

Simon, H.A. (1955) 'A behavioural model of rational choice', *Quarterly Journal of Economics* 69: 99–118.

Simon, H.A. (1956) 'Rational choice and the structure of the environment', *Psychological Review* 63(2): 129–38.

Sims, D.B.P. (1993) 'The formation of top managers: a discourse analysis of five managerial autobiographies', *British Journal of Management* 4: 57–68.

Sinetar, M. (1985) 'Entrepreneurs, chaos, and creativity – can creative people really survive large company structure?', *Sloan Management Review*, Winter: 57–62.

Singh, J.V., House, R.J. and Tucker, D.J. (1986) 'Organizational change and organizational mortality', *Administrative Science Quarterly* 31: 587–611.

Slevin, D.P. and Covin, J.G. (1990) 'Juggling entrepreneurial style and organizational structure – how to get your act together', *Sloan Management Review*, Winter: 43–53.

Sloan, A. (1963) *My Years with General Motors*, New York: Doubleday.

Smircich, L. and Stubbart, C. (1985) 'Strategic management in an enacted world', *Academy of Management Review* 10(4): 724–36.

Stalk, G. (1988) 'Time – the next source of competitive advantage', *Harvard Business Review* 66 (July–August): 41–51.

Stalk, G., Evans, P. and Shulman, L.E. (1992) 'Competing on capabilities: the new rules of corporate strategy', *Harvard Business Review* 70 (March–April): 57–69.

Starbuck, W.H. (1982) 'Congealing oil: inventing ideologies to justify acting ideologies out', *Journal of Management Studies* 19(1): 3–27.

Starbuck, W.H., Greve, A. and Hedberg, B.L.T. (1978) 'Responding to crises', *Journal of Business Administration* 9(2): 111–37.

Starrat, R.J. (1993) *The Drama of Leadership*, London: Falmer Press.

Stata, R. (1989) 'Organizational learning: the key to management innovation', *Sloan Management Review*, Spring: 63–74.

Staw, B. (1976) 'Knee-deep in the big muddy: a study of escalating commitment to a chosen course of action', *Organizational Behaviour and Human Performance* 16: 27–44.

Staw, B.M. and Ross, J. (1987) 'Knowing when to pull the plug', *Harvard Business Review* 65 (March–April): 68–74.

Steiner, G.A. (1979) *Strategic Planning: What Every Manager Must Know*, New York: Free Press.

Stevenson, H.H. and Harmeling, S. (1990) 'Entrepreneurial management's need for a more chaotic theory', *Journal of Business Venturing* 5: 1–14.

Stevenson, H.H. and Jarillo, J.C. (1986) 'Preserving entrepreneurship as companies grow', *Journal of Business Strategy* 6(5): 10–23.

Stewart, T.A. (1993) 'Welcome to the revolution', *Fortune*, 13 December: 32–8.

Stogdill, R.M. (1974) *Handbook of Leadership*, New York: Free Press.

Stopford, J.M. and Baden-Fuller, C. (1990) 'Corporate rejuvenation', *Journal of Management Studies* 27(4): 399–415.

Strebel, P. (1994) 'Choosing the right change path', *California Management Review*, Winter: 29–51.

Stukey, J. and White, D. (1993) 'When and when not to vertically integrate', *Sloan Management Review*, Spring: 71–83.

Tannenbaum, R. and Schmidt, W. (1958) 'How to choose a leadership pattern', *Harvard Business Review* 36: 95–101.

Taylor, W. (1991) 'The logic of global business: an interview with ABB's Percy Barnevik', *Harvard Business Review* 69 (March–April): 91–105.

Teece, D.J. (1986) 'Profiting from technological innovation: implications for integration, collaboration, licensing and public policy', *Research Policy* 15: 285–305.

Teng, J.T.C., Grover, V. and Fiedler, K.D. (1994) 'Business process reengineering: charting a strategic path for the information age', *California Management Review*, Spring: 9–31.

Thanheiser, H.T. (1972) 'Strategy and structure in German industrial enterprise', Doctoral dissertation, Harvard Business School.

Thomas, A.B. (1988) 'Does leadership make a difference to organizational performance?', *Administrative Science Quarterly* 33: 388–400.

Thompson, J.D. (1967) *Organizations in Action*, New York: McGraw-Hill.

Thorelli, H.B. (1986) 'Network: between markets and hierarchies', *Strategic Management Journal* 7: 37–51.

Tichy, N.M. and Charan, R. (1989) 'Speed, simplicity, self-confidence: an interview with Jack Welch', *Harvard Business Review* 67 (September–October): 112–20.

Tichy, N.M. and Devanna, M.A. (1986) *The Transformational Leader*, New York: Wiley.

Tunstall, W.B. (1986) 'The breakup of the Bell system: a case study in cultural transformation', *California Management Review* XXVIII(2), Winter: 110–24.

Tushman, M.L. and Anderson, P. (1986) 'Technological discontinuities and organizational environments', *Administrative Science Quarterly* 31: 439–65.

Tushman, M.L., Newman, W.H. and Romanelli, E. (1986) 'Convergence and upheaval: managing the unsteady pace of organizational evolution', *California Management Review* XXIX(1), Fall: 29–44.

Tyre, M.J. and Orlikowski, W.J. (1994) 'Windows of opportunity: temporal patterns of technological adaptation in organizations', *Organization Science* 5(1): 98–118.

Ulrich, D., Jick, T. and Von Glinnow, M.A. (1993) 'High-impact learning: building and diffusing learning capability', *Organizational Dynamics* 22 (Autumn): 52–66.

Uttal, B. (1985) 'Behind the fall of Steve Jobs', *Fortune*, 5 August: 12–16.

Utterback, J.M. (1994) *Mastering the Dynamics of Innovation*, Boston: Harvard Business School Press.

Utterback, J.M. and Abernathy, W.J. (1975) 'A dynamic model of process and product innovation', *Omega* 3(6): 639–56.

Vaill, P.B. (1989) *Managing as a Performing Art*, San Francisco: Jossey-Bass.

Venkatesan, R. (1992) 'Strategic sourcing: to make or not to make', *Harvard Business Review* 70 (November–December): 98–107.

Verity, J. (1992) 'Deconstructing the computer industry', *Business Week*, 23 November: 44–52.

Waterman, R.H., Peters, T.J. and Phillips, J.R. (1980) 'Structure is not organization', *Business Horizons* 23(3): 14–26.

Watkins, J., Skinner, C. and Pearson, J. (1993) 'Business process re-engineering: hype, hazard or heaven', *Business Change and Re-engineering* 1(2): 41–6.

Wernerfelt, B. (1984) 'A resource-based view of the firm', *Strategic Management Journal* 5: 171–80.

Westley, F. and Mintzberg, H. (1989) 'Visionary leadership and strategic management', *Strategic Management Journal* 10: 17–32.

Whittington, R. (1993) *What is Strategy – and Does it Matter?*, London: Routledge.

Wiersema, M. (1992) 'Strategic consequences of executive succession within diversified firms', *Journal of Management Studies* 29(1): 73–94.

Wiersema, M.F. and Hansen, G.S. (1993) 'Corporate strategy: a resource-based and product market approach', in H.E. Glass, B.N. Cavan and D. Willey (eds) *Handbook of Business Strategy* (1994 Yearbook), New York: Faulkner & Gray.

Williamson, O.E. (1975) *Markets and Hierarchies: Analysis and Antitrust Implications*, New York: Free Press.

Wrigley, L. (1970) 'Divisional autonomy and diversification', DBA dissertation, Harvard Business School.

Yukl, G. (1989) 'Managerial leadership: a review of theory and research', *Journal of Management* 15(2): 251–89.

Zajac, E.J. (1990) 'CEO selection, succession, compensation and firm performance: a theoretical integration and empirical analysis', *Strategic Management Journal* 11: 217–30.

Zaleznik, A. (1977) 'Managers and leaders: are they different?', *Harvard Business Review* 55 (May–June): 67–78.

Zaleznik, A. (1992) 'Managers and leaders: are they different?', *Harvard Business Review* 70 (March–April): 126–35 (HBR Classic reprint with retrospective commentary).

Zucker, L.G. (1987) 'Institutional theories of organization', *Annual Review of Sociology* 13: 443–64.

Name index

Subject index